Practical Backend Programming

Build Flask and FastAPI applications, asynchronous programming, containerization and deploy apps on cloud

Tim Peters

Copyright © 2024 by GitforGits

Published by: GitforGits

Publisher: Sonal Dhandre

www.gitforgits.com

support@gitforgits.com

Printed in India

First Printing: January 2024

ISBN: 9788119177615

Cover Design by: Kitten Publishing

For permission to use material from this book, please contact GitforGits at support@gitforgits.com.

Prologue

Welcome to "Practical Python Backend Programming." I'm Tim Peters, and in this book, I've simplified my years of software development experience to help you navigate the complex world of backend programming with Python. Whether you're a seasoned Python developer, a non-Python programmer venturing into Python's vast landscape, a full stack developer looking to improve your backend skills, or a new web developer starting out, this book is for you.

The challenges I faced as I transitioned from writing simple scripts to developing robust backend systems inspired me to write this book. I've learned over the years that the backend architecture is the foundation of any successful application. Data processing, security enforcement, and the business logic all take place here. As a result of Python's popularity as a top language for backend development, I saw a need for a resource that could walk developers through every step of the process.

This book begins with the fundamentals of creating a Python development environment optimized for backend development. You'll learn how to set up Python with the appropriate tools and libraries to improve your coding experience. From there, we'll delve deep into the heart of Python programming, where I'll help you master its syntax, data structures, and fundamental concepts, giving you a solid foundation to build on.

We then move on to more advanced topics like web development with popular frameworks like Flask and FastAPI. These chapters are intended to teach you not only how to build applications, but also about the structure and design patterns that result in scalable and maintainable code.

Since data is fundamental to backend programming, this book explores deeply into database management techniques. You'll work with relational databases like PostgreSQL and MySQL, as well as NoSQL options like MongoDB, to understand when and how to use them effectively. SQLAlchemy demonstrates how integrating an ORM can simplify database operations in your applications.

As applications grow, they need to handle more complex tasks like asynchronous operations and real-time data processing. Here, I'll show you how to do asynchronous programming in Python and real-time data handling with Kafka. You'll learn how to manage background tasks with Celery and build scalable applications that can handle large amounts of data without issue.

Security is critical, and this book provides a comprehensive look at how to secure your applications. From JWT and OAuth authentication to API endpoint security and SSL implementation, you'll learn how to effectively protect your application and data.

Finally, no modern backend book is complete without addressing deployment and scalability. You'll learn how to containerize your applications with Docker, manage them with Kubernetes, and deploy them to the cloud via AWS. I'll demonstrate how these technologies work together to create a continuous pipeline from development to deployment.

"Practical Python Backend Programming" is more than just a programming guide; it is a path to becoming a skilled backend developer capable of designing and deploying powerful and efficient applications. Join me on this journey and let's create some incredible things with Python.

Content

Preface

"Practical Python Backend Programming" is a quick pragmatic book that teaches both new and experienced developers the fundamentals of backend development with Python. All sorts of developers, from Python programmers to non-Python programmers, full stack developers, and web developers, will find what they need to know to become experts in backend programming in this entire book.

The book covers key topics in backend development, including how to set up stable development environments and how to use virtual environments for better dependency management. With this book, readers will have a firm grasp of Python programming with an emphasis on backend tasks by learning the language's syntax, data structures, and functions.

The book teaches you to create and launch dynamic web apps by providing an in-depth look at web frameworks such as Flask and FastAPI. It teaches SQLAlchemy for efficient data handling and advanced database integration, and it shows to improve applications with databases like PostgreSQL, MySQL, and MongoDB. Strategies for managing concurrent operations and improving performance are also covered in the book, along with asynchronous programming in Python.

Ensuring security is of utmost importance in backend development. This book delves into various authentication methods, secure communication protocols such as HTTPS, and techniques to secure REST APIs. For efficient management of asynchronous tasks and real-time data processing, it also introduces message brokers such as RabbitMQ and Kafka.

The book teaches its readers how to containerize apps and manage them on a large scale by integrating technologies like Docker and Kubernetes. It goes on to talk about how to use serverless architectures, how to use modern tools for continuous integration and deployment, and how to deploy apps to cloud platforms like AWS.

This book claims to teach its readers how to write efficient and readable Python code for robust backend systems and how to build, deploy, and maintain such systems.

In this book you will learn how to:

- Build dynamic web apps with strong backend logic using Flask and FastAPI.

- Write efficient, well-structured backend code by learning Python's syntax, functions, and best practices.

- Make your apps more efficient and scalable by using asynchronous programming techniques.

- Investigate Kubernetes and Docker to orchestrate and containerize apps for improved deployment and scalability.

- Use AWS's cloud services to deploy apps with guaranteed uptime and lightning-fast performance.

- Improve efficiency and compatibility by setting up and managing Python development environments.

- Enhance your data handling capabilities by learning to integrate and manipulate databases using SQLAlchemy.

- Protect online apps with OAuth and JWT's sophisticated authorization and authentication features.

- Efficiently process data in real-time and broker messages with RabbitMQ and Kafka.

- Streamline processes, cut down on mistakes, and implement continuous integration and deployment by following best practices.

GitforGits

Prerequisites

Whether you're a seasoned Python developer, a non-Python programmer stepping into Python's vast landscape, a full stack developer aiming to sharpen your backend skills, or a new web developer embarking on your programming journey, this book is crafted for you.

Codes Usage

Are you in need of some helpful code examples to assist you in your programming and documentation? Look no further! Our book offers a wealth of supplemental material, including code examples and exercises.

Not only is this book here to aid you in getting your job done, but you have our permission to use the example code in your programs and documentation. However, please note that if you are reproducing a significant portion of the code, we do require you to contact us for permission.

But don't worry, using several chunks of code from this book in your program or answering a question by citing our book and quoting example code does not require permission. But if you do choose to give credit, an attribution typically includes the title, author, publisher, and ISBN. For example, "Practical Python Backend Programming by Tim Peters".

If you are unsure whether your intended use of the code examples falls under fair use or the permissions outlined above, please do not hesitate to reach out to us at support@gitforgits.com.

We are happy to assist and clarify any concerns.

Acknowledgement

I owe a tremendous debt of gratitude to GitforGits, for their unflagging enthusiasm and wise counsel throughout the entire process of writing this book. Their knowledge and careful editing helped make sure the piece was useful for people of all reading levels and comprehension skills. In addition, I'd like to thank everyone involved in the publishing process for their efforts in making this book a reality. Their efforts, from copyediting to advertising, made the project what it is today.

Finally, I'd like to express my gratitude to everyone who has shown me unconditional love and encouragement throughout my life. Their support was crucial to the completion of this book. I appreciate your help with this endeavour and your continued interest in my career.

CHAPTER 1:
FUNDAMENTALS OF
BACKEND DEVELOPMENT

Introduction

In the opening chapter titled "Fundamentals of Backend Development," we embark on a journey to explore the essential components that make up the backbone of modern web applications. This chapter lays the groundwork for understanding what backend development entails and the pivotal role that Python plays in this landscape. We start by defining backend development, detailing the functionalities and processes that happen behind the scenes of a web application.

Next, we delve into why Python is a favored choice for backend development, learning its simplicity, flexibility, and the robust ecosystem of frameworks and libraries that support it. To equip you with the necessary tools, we walk through setting up a development environment that includes Python, Visual Studio Code, and Linux. This setup ensures that you have a solid and consistent platform for developing backend applications.

We then introduce the concept of virtual environments, which are crucial for managing dependencies and avoiding conflicts between projects. As command-line proficiency is vital for backend developers, we cover the basics of the Command Line Interface (CLI), providing you with the skills to navigate and operate your system efficiently.

Version control is another cornerstone of professional development, and we introduce you to Git, the most widely used system for tracking changes and collaborating in software projects. To refresh and solidify your Python skills, we review fundamental concepts such as syntax, data structures, and functions—ensuring you're well-prepared to handle backend tasks.

Finally, we round off the chapter with best practices in Python programming. These guidelines help you write clean, maintainable, and efficient code, forming good habits early on in your backend development career. This chapter is designed to establish a robust foundation, enabling you to build more complex and dynamic backend systems in the subsequent chapters.

Overview of Backend Development

The backend of a web application, often referred to as the server-side, is a fundamental component of web development that focuses on the logic, database interactions, user authentication, and server configuration. It works behind the scenes to manage the vital functions that are not visible to users but crucial for the functioning of the application. We shall now explore the essential components of any backend web application and their roles in a typical web environment.

Essential Components of Backend Development

Server

In the context of web applications, a server can be understood as both software and hardware. Hardware-wise, a server is a computer designed to process requests and deliver data to other computers over a local network or the Internet. Compared to regular computers, server hardware is optimized to handle more demanding tasks, offer greater storage capacity, and manage network traffic efficiently. They must also be highly reliable, available, and scalable, coping with varying loads and functioning continuously without failure.

Software-wise, a server refers to the application or service running on this hardware, waiting to handle requests from clients. This includes web servers, mail servers, and file servers, among others. The most common type of server in web development is a web server.

Web servers are specifically designed to store, process, and deliver web pages to users. They handle HTTP requests from clients, which can be browsers or other web-based applications.

Given below is how they function step-by-step:

- The server listens for requests sent over the Internet to a specific IP address and port. Once a request is received, the server reads and interprets the HTTP headers to determine the nature of the request.

- Depending on the request's requirements (such as retrieving a webpage, querying a database, or submitting form data), the server performs the necessary operations. This may involve running server-side scripts or querying databases to fetch or update data.

- Web servers often need to load resources that make up web pages, including HTML files, CSS for styling, JavaScript files, and media files. These files are often stored on the server and must be retrieved quickly to ensure a responsive user experience.

- For dynamic pages that require backend processing (like PHP, Python scripts, or Java), the server executes these scripts to generate HTML based on the current state of the database or the server's business logic.

- After processing the request and fetching all necessary data, the server packages everything into an HTTP response and sends it back to the client. This response could be a complete HTML page, a JSON/XML data set for APIs, or a status message about the outcome of the request.

Database

A database is an organized collection of data stored and accessed electronically from a computer system. Databases are designed to offer an efficient, reliable, and convenient way to store and retrieve multiple data types. The database management system (DBMS) serves as the interface between the database and the end users or application programs, ensuring that data is organized and maintained without redundancy and inconsistency.

Following are the core functions of databases in backend development:

- Databases provide a systematic and organized way of storing data such that it can be retrieved and manipulated efficiently. Data organization involves categorizing and indexing the data, where indexing helps in quick search and retrieval.

- Through the use of queries, databases allow you to fetch data dynamically. This is crucial for serving user-specific content, performing statistical analyses, and generating reports.

- Databases allow the insertion, modification, and deletion of data stored within. This is essential for maintaining an accurate and up-to-date record of information that reflects real-time interactions with the application.

- Many databases support ACID (Atomicity, Consistency, Isolation, Durability) properties to ensure that all transactions are processed reliably. This means that the database ensures all operations within a transaction are completed successfully before committing the transaction. If an error occurs, the transaction is aborted and the database is left unchanged.

- Databases manage multiple users accessing and manipulating the data concurrently without interference, using locks or by providing multiple versions of data.

Application Programming Interfaces (API)

An API can be thought of as a contract between a provider and a user of a service. The provider agrees to supply the service as per the specifications laid out in the API documentation, and the user agrees to interact with the service strictly according to those specifications. APIs are implemented by function calls composed of verbs and nouns. The nouns are the resources, and the verbs are the actions to be performed on those resources.

Following are the types of APIs in web development:

- Web APIs: These are designed for both the server-side and the client-side, allowing interaction over the web. This interaction is typically done over HTTP, making it easy for web systems to communicate. REST and GraphQL are the most popular types of web APIs.

- Internal APIs: These are used within an organization to integrate different internal systems and services. They are not exposed outside of the organization, providing an added layer of security and allowing for customized functionalities that are specific to the business's needs.

- External APIs: Made available to external users, allowing third-party developers to access features or resources of a tool or service. These APIs need robust documentation and heightened security measures to manage how external parties can interact with the system.

- Third-party APIs: These are APIs provided by third parties, typically enabling services like payments processing, social media interactions, or data feeds (for example, APIs provided by PayPal, Twitter, or Google Maps).

Web Framework

A web framework is a software framework designed to support the development of web applications including web services, web resources, and web APIs. Frameworks provide libraries and tools to help developers build applications faster and more efficiently by automating standard processes.

Most web frameworks offer several key components:

- Routing: Determines how incoming HTTP requests are directed to the appropriate handlers. Developers define routes using patterns and specify which functions are called based on the incoming URL, often with support for dynamic URL parameters.

- Request and Response Objects: Frameworks simplify the handling of HTTP requests and responses by wrapping these in objects. This provides a simple interface for developers to access data and manipulate the type of response returned to the client.

- Template Engine: Template engines allow developers to build dynamic HTML pages by embedding backend logic (like loops, conditionals, and variable data) into HTML. It separates the design and code, making the web applications easier to manage and modify.

- Database Integration: Web frameworks often come with built-in or add-on ORM (Object-Relational Mapping) tools that abstract database interactions. This allows developers to work with databases using the programming language constructs instead of writing SQL queries directly.

- Middleware Support: Middleware are hooks or services that can be executed before or after a request is processed. This is useful for implementing functionalities that need to be processed in every request, such as user authentication, data sanitization, and session management.

- Security Features: Frameworks provide security features to protect web applications from common vulnerabilities such as SQL injection, Cross-site Scripting (XSS), and Cross-Site Request Forgery (CSRF). They handle these through various forms of input sanitization, secure defaults, and other best practices.

Middleware

Middleware is software that lies between an application and the network or the system on which it runs. It connects different components of an application or different applications altogether, facilitating communication and data management. Middleware services can include messaging services, authentication, content management, API management, and more.

Middleware is often learned in the context of specific frameworks that make it a central part of their architecture. Following are a few examples:

- Express.js Middleware: In the Express.js framework (Node.js), middleware functions are functions that have access to the request object (req), the response object (res), and the next middleware function in the application's request-response cycle. These functions can execute any code, make changes to the request and response objects, end the request-response cycle, and call the next middleware function.

- Django Middleware: In Django (Python), middleware is a lightweight plugin that processes during request and response execution. Django maintains a list of middleware to execute during requests and responses, and each must be designed to be compatible with the other middleware in the chain.

- ASP.NET Core Middleware: In ASP.NET Core, middleware components are assembled into an application pipeline to handle requests and responses. Each component can perform operations before and after the next component in the pipeline.

Caching

Caching is the process of storing data in a cache, a high-speed data storage layer, so that future requests for that data can be served faster. The data stored in a cache might be the result of an earlier computation or a duplicate of data stored elsewhere. When a request is made for data that is cached, the system can bypass the slower backend processes and deliver the response quickly.

The general process of caching involves several steps:

- A user or client application makes a request for data.

- The system checks if the requested data is in the cache.

- If the data is cached ("cache hit"), it is returned immediately, skipping the slower data retrieval processes. If the data is not in the cache ("cache miss"), the request is processed normally, and the data is retrieved from the slower backend or storage system.

After a cache miss, once the data is retrieved, it is stored in the cache so that any future requests for the same data can be served faster.

To manage memory and ensure the cache does not become outdated, older or less frequently accessed data is periodically removed from the cache. Algorithms like Least Recently Used (LRU) or First In First Out (FIFO) are often used for this purpose.

Functioning of Backend Components

When a user interacts with a front-end application, such as by clicking on a link or submitting a form, the request is sent to the server via the internet.

Given below is how all the above discussed components interact with each other:

- Request Handling: The server, running a web framework, receives the request. The web framework routes the request to the appropriate controller based on the URL and the request type (GET, POST, etc.).

- Middleware Processing: Before the request reaches the controller, it may pass through various middleware. This can handle tasks like logging, user authentication, and data validation. Middleware can reject requests, requiring no further processing, or pass them along the system.

- Business Logic Execution: Once the request reaches the controller, the server executes the business logic, which might involve querying or updating the database through an ORM (Object Relational Mapping) or directly using SQL queries.

- API Interaction: If the application relies on external services, the server might make API calls to external systems to retrieve data or perform operations. This interaction is often asynchronous and needs to be handled carefully to maintain performance.

- Data Response: After processing, the server prepares the response, which might include fetching data from the cache to speed up response time. The response is sent back to the client, either as HTML, JSON, or XML.

- Client Update: The client (browser or mobile app) receives the response and updates the user interface accordingly. If the response is data (usually in JSON format), the front-end will use it to update the application's state or render it as needed.

Backend development is a complex and critical component of web development that requires a good understanding of server technologies, database management, middleware, API development, and caching mechanisms. Mastery of these elements ensures the creation of robust, efficient, and scalable web applications.

Role of Python in Backend Development

Python has emerged as a leading player in backend development due to its simplicity, versatility, and robust ecosystem. In the domain of web development, Python's role is characterized by its ability to accommodate the rapid development of applications, handle a variety of backend tasks, and integrate with various systems and technologies. This multifaceted applicability makes Python a preferred choice for developers looking to build reliable, scalable, and maintainable backend systems.

Versatility and Readability

Python's syntax is clear and concise, which makes it an excellent choice for backend development. Its readability ensures that even complex systems are easy to understand and maintain, reducing the potential for errors and simplifying the debugging process. This ease of use extends to writing and deploying server-side code, where Python's straightforward syntax allows developers to express concepts without writing additional code. For example, Python's use of white space and common expressions allows developers to focus more on logic than on syntax formalities, speeding up the development process.

Comprehensive Standard Library

Python's extensive standard library is one of its greatest strengths, providing modules and packages for almost any programming task. This includes a variety of server-side functionalities such as database access, file handling, inter-process communications, and even internet protocols like HTTP and FTP. This wide range of supported operations makes Python a versatile tool for backend developers, who can use its standard library to perform a multitude of backend tasks efficiently without the need for third-party modules.

Frameworks and Tools for Backend Development

Python's ecosystem includes several powerful frameworks and tools specifically tailored for backend development, which help in quickly building robust web applications. Popular frameworks include:

- Django: Known for its "batteries-included" approach, Django comes with numerous built-in features such as an ORM (Object-Relational Mapping), authentication mechanisms, and message passing facilities, all of which are indispensable for modern web applications. Django's structure promotes the rapid development of high-quality web applications.

- Flask: As a microframework, Flask provides the bare essentials to get a web application running. Its simplicity and flexibility make it suitable for small to medium-sized applications and for developers who prefer to add extensions based on their specific project requirements.

- FastAPI: FastAPI is a modern, fast (high-performance) web framework for building APIs with Python 3.7+ based on standard Python type hints. The key features of FastAPI include fast to run, fast to code, and fewer bugs.

Asynchronous Support

Python 3.5 introduced native support for asynchronous programming through **asyncio**, a library that allows for asynchronous I/O operations. Asynchronous support is critical in handling large volumes of data and requests, which is common in modern web applications. This is particularly useful in improving the efficiency and performance of I/O-bound and network-bound applications. Frameworks like FastAPI and Sanic are designed to take full advantage of Python's asynchronous capabilities, enabling developers to handle more connections and data with less hardware.

Integration Capabilities

Python excels in its ability to integrate with other languages and technologies. This is crucial in backend development, where applications often need to interact with legacy systems, utilize third-party services, and perform data analysis. Python's compatibility with C/C++ and its ability to run on virtually all operating systems make it a highly flexible choice for backend systems. Additionally, Python's numerous libraries and APIs for data interaction make it straightforward to integrate complex functionalities into any application.

Database Connectivity

Python supports various databases, from traditional relational databases like MySQL and PostgreSQL to modern NoSQL databases like MongoDB and Cassandra. Libraries such as SQLAlchemy and Django's ORM allow for efficient database management and operations, abstracting a lot of the database handling and interactions, thus making database integration simpler and more robust.

Community and Resources

Python benefits immensely from a vibrant community of developers who contribute to a vast array of libraries and frameworks. This community not only drives the language's development forward but also provides tremendous support through documentation, forums, tutorials, and third-party packages. Whether a developer is facing a common problem or looking for a specialized library, chances are high that there's already a Python package out there to meet their needs.

Use in AI and Machine Learning

Python is also the leading language in artificial intelligence (AI) and machine learning (ML), fields that are increasingly pertinent to backend systems, especially in scenarios involving data processing, predictive analysis, and automated decision-making. Libraries like TensorFlow, PyTorch, and Scikit-learn are extensively used in the backend for analyzing user data and enhancing dynamic decision processes.

Python's role in backend development is significant due to its simplicity, a wide array of frameworks and libraries, asynchronous capabilities, database support, and strong community backing. These above characteristics make Python an adaptable, powerful, and efficient choice for developers building the backbone of modern web applications.

Setting up Development Environment: Python, VS Code, and Linux

Installing Linux

Assuming you are setting up a fresh development environment, the first step is to install Linux. Ubuntu, a popular Linux distribution, is well-supported and user-friendly, making it a great choice for developers.

- Visit the official Ubuntu website and download the latest LTS (Long Term Support) version.
- Use tools like Rufus or Etcher to create a bootable USB drive with the Ubuntu ISO file.
- Insert the USB drive into your computer, reboot, and enter your BIOS setup. Change the boot order to start from the USB drive, save changes, and exit. Follow the installation prompts of Ubuntu, selecting your preferences for language, keyboard layout, and partitioning.

Installing Python

Ubuntu comes with Python pre-installed, but it might not always be the latest version. To install the latest version of Python, you can use the terminal:

- Press **Ctrl+Alt+T** to open a terminal window.
- Run **sudo apt update** to update the package list.
- Install Python by executing **sudo apt install python3**.
- Check the installed version by typing **python3 --version**.

Installing Visual Studio Code (VS Code)

VS Code is a lightweight but powerful source code editor that supports Python development natively and can be enhanced via extensions.

Download VS Code: Go to the official Visual Studio Code website and download the .deb package (for Debian/Ubuntu).

Install VS Code:

- Open your terminal.
- Navigate to the directory where you downloaded the VS Code **.deb** file.
- Install the package using **sudo dpkg -i code_*.deb** (replace ***** with the version number).
- Resolve dependencies (if any) by running **sudo apt -f install**.

- You can start VS Code from your applications menu or by typing **code** in your terminal.

Configuring VS Code for Python

To effectively develop Python applications using VS Code, configure it with necessary extensions and settings:

Install Python Extension for VS Code:

- Open VS Code.

- Go to the Extensions view by clicking on the square icon on the sidebar or pressing **Ctrl+Shift+X**.

- Search for "Python" and install the extension provided by Microsoft.

Configure the Python Interpreter:

- Open a Python file or create a new one.

- Press **Ctrl+Shift+P** to open the Command Palette.

- Type "Python: Select Interpreter" and select the appropriate Python version that you installed on your system.

Setting Up a Virtual Environment

Virtual environments in Python allow you to manage dependencies for different projects separately. You can create a virtual environment using the following steps:

Install virtualenv:

- Install **virtualenv** by running **pip install virtualenv**.

Create a Virtual Environment:

- Navigate to your project directory in the terminal.

- Run **virtualenv venv** (where **venv** is the name of the virtual environment).

Activate the Virtual Environment:

- On Linux, activate it by running **source venv/bin/activate**.

- Your prompt will change to indicate that you are working within the **venv**.

Deactivate:

- Exit the virtual environment by running **deactivate** when you are done working.

Final Steps and Testing

Now that you have your development environment set up with Linux, Python, and VS Code, it's time to test it by creating a simple Python application.

Create a Test File:

- In VS Code, create a new file named **test.py**.

- Write a simple Python script, for example: **print("Hello, World!")**

Run the Test File:

- Open a terminal in VS Code by pressing **Ctrl+`** (backtick).

- Make sure your virtual environment is activated.

- Run the script by typing **python test.py**.

You should see "Hello, World!" printed in the terminal, indicating that your Python setup is correct and operational. This environment is now ready for more complex backend development tasks, including web application development with frameworks like Django or Flask.

Introduction to Virtual Environments

What is a Virtual Environment?

A virtual environment is an isolated workspace that allows Python libraries to be installed in a directory without affecting the global Python installation. This is particularly useful when different projects require different versions of the same package, as it prevents version conflicts. Each virtual environment has its own Python binary (which matches the version of the Python interpreter used to create it) and can have its own independent set of installed Python packages in its site directories.

Why use Virtual Environments?

The main reasons for using virtual environments in Python development are:

- Virtual environments allow you to manage dependencies required by different projects by creating isolated spaces for them. This means that you can have different versions of a library for different projects without them clashing.

- Using a virtual environment ensures that all developers working on a project have the same dependencies, which reduces "works on my machine" problems.

- By having all project dependencies isolated in a virtual environment, it becomes easier to understand what exactly needs to be deployed with the application, reducing the chances of missing modules.

- Virtual environments make it safe to experiment with different packages and update package versions without the risk of affecting other development work.

How to Setup and use Virtual Environments?

Setting up a virtual environment involves a few straightforward steps:

Installation

The **venv** module is the standard tool for creating virtual environments in Python 3, and it comes pre-installed. For Python 2, **virtualenv** must be installed separately.

Creating Virtual Environment

- For Python 3, navigate to your project's directory in the terminal and run:

```
python3 -m venv myenv
```

- Replace **myenv** with the name of your virtual environment.
- For Python 2, after installing **virtualenv**, you would use:

```
virtualenv myenv
```

Activating Virtual Environment

On Linux or macOS, activate the virtual environment by running:

```
source myenv/bin/activate
```

When activated, the virtual environment's name will typically appear in parentheses in your terminal prompt, indicating that any Python or pip commands will only affect this environment.

Installing Packages

Once the environment is activated, you can install packages as usual with pip:

```
pip install package_name
```

Deactivating

To stop using a virtual environment and return to the global Python environment, simply run:

```
deactivate
```

Managing Dependencies

To keep track of a project's dependencies, you can create a **requirements.txt** file by running:

```
pip freeze > requirements.txt
```

This file can then be used to install all the necessary packages in another environment or on another machine:

```
pip install -r requirements.txt
```

Best Practices

- Create a new virtual environment for each project to keep dependencies required by different projects separate.

- It's a good practice to include your **requirements.txt** in your version control system, but exclude the virtual environment directory (**myenv/**) to avoid uploading a large number of files to your repository.

- Keep the packages within virtual environments up to date to take advantage of recent bug fixes and enhancements.

More advanced tools such as **pipenv** and **poetry** provide additional features for dependency management. These tools automatically manage a virtual environment for your projects and handle dependency resolution in a more sophisticated way, providing lock files to ensure that the environments are reproducible. These tools are particularly useful in production scenarios where consistency across different systems and deployments is crucial.

Basics of Command Line Interface (CLI)

The Command Line Interface (CLI) is an essential tool for developers, especially when managing the development environment for backend web applications. It allows for powerful, quick, and flexible interaction with the computer, using text-based commands rather than graphical interfaces. Mastering the CLI can significantly enhance productivity and efficiency, and is particularly useful in environments like Linux, where many development tasks can be more efficiently handled through the command line.

Understanding the CLI

The CLI involves entering commands into a terminal or command prompt to perform specific tasks, such as navigating the filesystem, managing files and directories, installing software, or controlling system processes. These commands are processed by the shell, a program that interprets commands and acts as an intermediary between the user and the operating system.

Basic CLI Commands

Following are some fundamental commands that are essential for navigating and managing the filesystem on a Linux-based system, which will be your development environment:

pwd (Print Working Directory):

- This command displays the current directory you are in, helping you understand your location within the filesystem.

ls (List):

- Use this command to list all files and directories in the current directory.

- **ls -l** provides a detailed list, including file permissions, number of links, owner, group, size, and date of last modification.

- **ls -a** lists all entries including those starting with a dot, which are hidden by default.

cd (Change Directory):

- This command changes the current directory.

- **cd /path/to/directory** moves you to the specified directory.

- **cd ..** moves you up one directory level.

- **cd** or **cd ~** takes you back to your home directory.

mkdir (Make Directory):

- Creates a new directory.

- **mkdir new_directory** creates a new directory named **new_directory** in the current location.

rmdir (Remove Directory):

- Deletes an empty directory.

- **rmdir old_directory** removes the directory named **old_directory** if it is empty.

rm (Remove):

- Removes files or directories.
- **rm file.txt** deletes the file **file.txt**.
- **rm -r directory** recursively deletes the directory named **directory** and all its contents.

touch (Create File):

- Creates a new, empty file or updates the timestamp of an existing file.
- **touch filename** creates a new file named **filename** or updates its last modified time if it exists.

nano, **vim**, **emacs** (Text Editors):

- Open files in a text editor right from the command line.
- **nano file.txt**, **vim file.txt**, and **emacs file.txt** open **file.txt** in Nano, Vim, and Emacs respectively.

cat (Concatenate):

- Displays the content of files to the terminal.
- **cat file.txt** prints the contents of **file.txt** on the screen.

cp (Copy):

- Copies files or directories.
- cp source_file destination_file copies source_file to destination_file.
- cp -r source_directory destination_directory recursively copies a directory.

mv (Move):

- Moves or renames files or directories.
- **mv old_name new_name** renames a file or directory from **old_name** to **new_name**.

grep (Global Regular Expression Print):

- Searches for patterns in files using regular expressions.

- **grep 'pattern' file.txt** searches for 'pattern' in **file.txt** and prints lines where the pattern is found.

chmod (Change Mode):

- Changes the file permissions.

- **chmod 755 file.txt** sets the permissions of **file.txt** to read, write, and execute for the owner, and read and execute for group and others.

chown (Change Owner):

- Changes the owner and/or group of a file or directory.

- **chown user:group file.txt** changes the owner to **user** and the group to **group** for **file.txt**.

Tips for using CLI

- Use the Tab key to auto-complete file and directory names. This can save time and reduce errors in typing.

- Use the up and down arrow keys to scroll through previously entered commands, making it easy to repeat or modify earlier commands.

- Use pipes (**|**) and redirection (**>**, **>>**) to direct the output from one command to another or into a file, combining commands to perform complex tasks efficiently.

When working in a Linux environment, you may significantly simplify your backend development workflow by using these fundamental CLI commands. It offers a strong means of automating processes, managing the system, and completing jobs rapidly.

Introduction to Version Control with Git

Version control systems are a critical component of the software development process, enabling developers to manage changes to source code over time. This tool is essential for collaboration, allowing multiple people to work on the same codebase without conflict, and it provides a history of changes which can be helpful for debugging and understanding project evolution. Among the various version control systems available, Git is one of the most popular and widely used due to its efficiency, flexibility, and powerful branching capabilities.

Introduction to Version Control and Git

Version Control: At its core, version control is the practice of tracking and managing changes to software code. Version control systems allow multiple developers to work simultaneously on a single project. Each developer works on their own copy of the code, and their changes are merged into a shared repository. This ensures that there is a comprehensive record of who made which changes and when, allowing for specific changes to be traced or even rolled back if necessary.

Git: Developed by Linus Torvalds in 2005, Git is a distributed version control system. Unlike centralized version control systems, every Git directory on every computer is a full-fledged repository with complete history and full version tracking capabilities, independent of network access or a central server. Git is especially known for its robustness, speed, and efficiency in handling small to very large projects.

Basic Git Operations for Backend Development

Getting started with Git involves a few foundational commands and concepts that are essential for everyday development tasks:

Installing Git

- On Linux, you can install Git from the terminal by running **sudo apt-get install git**.
- Verify the installation by typing **git --version**.

Configuring Git

- Set your user name and email address because Git embeds this information into each commit you do. You can set these with the following commands:

```
--global user.name "Your Name"
```

```
git config --global user.email
"your.email@gitforgits.com"
```

Initializing Repository

- Navigate to your project directory in the command line and type **git init**. This command creates a new subdirectory named **.git** that houses all of your necessary repository files — a Git repository skeleton. A new root commit is also initialized.

Cloning Repository

- To copy an existing Git repository hosted somewhere like GitHub, use:

```
git clone https://github.com/username/repository.git
```

- This command creates a directory with all the files and complete revision history.

Adding and Committing Files

- Use **git add <filename>** to stage changes for a specific file, or **git add .** to stage all changes in the directory.

- Commit staged files using **git commit -m "Commit message"**, where the message explains what changes were made.

Branching and Merging

- Branches are used to develop features isolated from each other. The master branch is the "default" branch when you create a repository.

- Create a new branch with git branch new-branch-name and switch to it with git checkout new-branch-name.

- After development, merge it back to the main branch (e.g., master) with **git checkout master** followed by **git merge new-branch-name**.

Pushing Changes

- To send your commits to a remote repository, use **git push origin master**, where 'origin' is the default name for your remote repository and 'master' is your branch.

Pulling Updates

- To fetch and merge changes from the remote repository to your local machine, use **git pull**.

Handling Merge Conflicts

- Conflicts occur when merging branches with competing changes. Git will prompt you to resolve conflicts manually by editing the files and then running **git add <file>** to indicate conflict resolution.

Using the Git Log

- The **git log** command shows the chronological commit history for the current branch.

- Use **git log --oneline** for a brief history view.

By integrating Git into your development workflow, you will be able to more effectively manage the progress of your project. For every backend development project, Git is more than just a safety net; it's a strong tool for collaboration and change management.

Python Refresher: Syntax, Data Structures, and

Functions

Python Syntax

Python is renowned for its readability and simplicity, making it an excellent choice for beginners and experienced developers alike. Python's syntax is intuitive and closer to human language, which is part of its appeal.

Following are some key aspects:

Indentation

Python uses whitespace to define scope; such as the scope of loops, functions, and classes. Other programming languages often use curly brackets for this purpose. This requirement for indentation helps make Python code very readable.

```python
if 10 > 5:
  print("10 is greater than 5")
```

Variables

Variables in Python are created when you assign a value to them. Python is dynamically-typed, which means you do not need to declare the type of variable while declaring it.

```python
x = 5
y = "Hello, World!"
```

Comments

Python uses the hash (**#**) character to start writing a comment.

```python
# This is a comment
print("Hello, World!")
```

Data Structures

Python offers several built-in data structures that are robust and feature-rich. Following are the most commonly used:

Lists

Ordered and changeable collections that allow duplicate members.

```python
fruits = ["apple", "banana", "cherry"]

print(fruits[1]) # Output: banana

fruits.append("orange") # Adds "orange" to the end of the
list
```

Tuples

Ordered and unchangeable collections that allow duplicate members. Tuples are written with round brackets.

```python
thistuple = ("apple", "banana", "cherry")

print(thistuple[1]) # Output: banana
```

Sets

Unordered, unindexed collections with no duplicate members. Great for membership testing and eliminating duplicate entries.

```python
thisset = {"apple", "banana", "cherry"}

print("banana" in thisset) # Output: True
```

Dictionaries

Unordered, changeable, and indexed collections with no duplicate members. They have keys and values.

```python
thisdict = {
 "brand": "Ford",
 "model": "Mustang",
 "year": 1964
}
```

```
print(thisdict["model"]) # Output: Mustang
```

Functions

Functions are a key way to segment your Python code into modules, making it more readable and reusable. They are defined using the **def** keyword.

Defining a Function

Following is how you can define a Python function:

```
def greet(name):
  return "Hello, " + name
```

Calling a Function

To call the function, use the function name followed by parentheses.

```
message = greet("Alice")
print(message) # Output: Hello, Alice
```

Parameters

Functions can take parameters, which are specified after the function name inside the parentheses. You can also define default parameter values.

```
def greet(name, greeting="Hello"):
  return greeting + ", " + name
```

Keyword Arguments

When calling functions, you can use keyword arguments to ensure that each argument is matched with its corresponding parameter, even if they are not in order.

```
print(greet(name="Bob", greeting="Hi")) # Output: Hi, Bob
```

Arbitrary Arguments

If you do not know how many arguments will be passed to your function, add a ***** before the parameter name in the function definition.

```python
def make_smoothie(*fruits):
  for fruit in fruits:
  print("Adding:", fruit)
make_smoothie("apple", "banana", "cherry")
```

Lambda Functions

Small anonymous functions defined with the **lambda** keyword. Lambda functions can have any number of arguments but only one expression.

```python
double = lambda x: x * 2
print(double(5)) # Output: 10
```

Error Handling

Error handling in Python is done through the use of exceptions. A block of code that might cause an error can be put inside a **try** block. The **except** block contains code that handles the error.

```python
try:
 print(x)
except NameError:
 print("Variable x is not defined")
except:
 print("Something else went wrong")
```

Modules and Packages

Modules in Python are simply Python files with the **.py** extension containing Python code that can be imported into other Python files. To group multiple modules together, Python uses packages, which are directories containing a special file called **__init__.py**.

Importing Modules

You can use **import** to bring in any Python file as a module.

```
import math
print(math.sqrt(16)) # Output: 4.0
```

Importing with Aliases

You can create an alias when you import a module by using the **as** keyword.

```
import datetime as dt
today = dt.date.today()
```

From...Import Statement

If you only need specific items from a module, you can use **from** to import those directly into your namespace.

```
from math import sqrt
print(sqrt(16)) # Output: 4.0
```

Gaining a solid grasp of these Python fundamentals will enable you to construct backend applications with more strength and efficiency. It is essential for developers to have a strong understanding of these features in Python, whether it's for managing data using the built-in structures, constructing functions to encapsulate functionality, or handling errors and exceptions.

Best Practices in Python Programming

Adhering to best practices in Python programming is crucial for writing efficient, readable, and maintainable code, especially in backend development where complexity and scalability issues often arise. Following are some of the most important Python programming best practices.

Follow the Zen of Python

The Zen of Python is a collection of aphorisms that capture the philosophy of Python. You can view it by typing **import this** in your Python interpreter. It emphasizes simplicity, readability, and the notion of "one obvious way to do it," which helps in making the code intuitive and easy to maintain.

Adhere to PEP 8

PEP 8 is the style guide for Python code. It provides conventions on how Python code should be formatted and written, covering aspects like naming conventions, indentation, line length, whitespaces, imports organization, and comments. Following PEP 8 improves code readability and consistency, which is vital in a collaborative environment.

Indentation: Use 4 spaces per indentation level.

Line Length: Limit lines to 79 characters.

Naming Conventions: Use **CamelCase** for classes, **snake_case** for functions and variables, and **UPPER_CASE** for constants.

Write Docstrings

Docstrings are essential for documenting Python classes, methods, functions, and modules. They are written in triple quotes and appear right after the definition of a function, method, or class.

```python
def greet(name):
    """

    Greet a person with their name.


    Parameters:

    name (str): The name of the person to greet.


    Returns:

    str: A greeting message.
    """

    return f"Hello, {name}!"
```

Using docstrings helps other developers understand what the code does without diving into the details, facilitating better collaboration and maintenance.

Use Python's Built-in Functions and Libraries

Python comes with a rich standard library and many built-in functions that can help you perform common tasks more efficiently. Leveraging these can lead to faster, cleaner, and more efficient code.

- Functions like **map()**, **filter()**, **sum()**, **min()**, **max()** can often replace manual loops and are usually more performant.

- Before writing your own implementation, check if there's a library function. For example, use **json** for JSON parsing, **datetime** for date manipulations, or **os** and **sys** for system-related operations.

Utilize List Comprehensions and Generator Expressions

List comprehensions and generator expressions provide a concise and readable way to create lists or iterators. They are more straightforward and faster than using a loop to create lists.

```
# List comprehension

squares = [x**2 for x in range(10)]
```

```
# Generator expression

sum_of_squares = sum(x**2 for x in range(10))
```

Error Handling with Exceptions

Proper error handling is crucial for building reliable applications. Python uses exceptions for handling errors, and using them correctly can prevent your application from crashing and provide useful error messages to the user or developer.

- Use specific exceptions rather than a general **except:** clause.

- Use **try-except** blocks to catch potential errors.

- Always clean up resources using **finally** or a context manager.

```
try:

 process_file(file)

except FileNotFoundError:
```

```
    print("File does not exist")
finally:
    file.close()
```

Use Context Managers for Resource Management

Python's context managers are significant for managing resources, such as file streams, which need to be properly closed after their use is complete. Using the **with** statement ensures that resources are cleaned up promptly.

```
with open('example.txt', 'r') as file:
    contents = file.read()
```

Keep Functions Small and Focused

Each function should have a single, well-defined responsibility. This makes them reusable, testable, and easier to debug. If a function is trying to do too much, consider breaking it down into smaller functions.

Avoid Premature Optimization

While it's important to write efficient code, avoid premature optimization. First, write code that is clear and correct. Then, use profiling tools to find bottlenecks and optimize those specific parts of your code.

Use Version Control

Using a version control system like Git not only helps in managing the codebase changes but also in documenting the why behind code changes through commit messages. It's essential for collaboration and maintaining the code history.

Test your Code

Testing is critical for ensuring your code behaves as expected. Utilize Python's **unittest** or third-party libraries like **pytest** to write tests that validate each part of your application.

```
import unittest

class TestSum(unittest.TestCase):
```

```
def test_sum(self):

self.assertEqual(sum([1, 2, 3]), 6, "Should be 6")


if __name__ == '__main__':

unittest.main()
```

It is possible for Python developers to ensure that their software is not only functional but also clean, maintainable, and easy to comprehend if they adhere to certain best practices. Because the system's complexity might increase dramatically with the addition of new features, this is of the utmost importance while developing the backend.

Summary

In this chapter, we covered the groundwork for building Python backends. To start, we defined backend development and explained why Python is so useful for it because of its simplicity and resilience. We covered all the bases when it came to configuring the development environment, including installing Visual Studio Code and Python and configuring Linux to make a productive workspace out of these tools. We also looked into virtual environment design and maintenance to handle project-specific dependencies conflict-free.

Practical experience with the command line interface (CLI) was also thoroughly learned. In this section, you will find important commands for managing file systems and running programs. For backend development, these are crucial. Then, we explored Git, a version control system, and learned its benefits for managing project versions and team collaboration. Create a repository, make changes, work with branches, and merge code—all of which are important skills for readers to have in order to maintain a codebase organized. Finally, to ensure that you have a solid foundation in programming, we went over the syntax, data structures, and functions of Python once more. The chapter also went over some of the best practices for working with Python, particularly with regards to writing code that is efficient, well-structured, and simple to maintain. The use of meaningful docstrings, proper handling of errors and exceptions, and the utilization of Python's built-in functions are all instances of these best practices in action.

This chapter gave a comprehensive rundown of everything you need to know to set up a Python-based backend development environment, from the tools and methodologies to the best practices for coding and examples of well-built backend applications. Later chapters cover more advanced topics, but this foundational material lays the groundwork for them.

CHAPTER 2: BUILDING YOUR FIRST WEB APPLICATION WITH FLASK

Introduction

This chapter takes you on a hands-on tour of building a web project with Flask, a robust and lightweight Python web framework. The goal of this chapter is to give a thorough overview of the features and components that are necessary to construct a web application from scratch. First, we'll give you the rundown on Flask, covering the foundations and how its simplicity and versatility make it a go-to for rapid web app development. The next step is to prepare a Flask environment, which includes installing the required libraries and tools to begin developing your application.

You will master the fundamentals of web application routing and views, including how to handle various URLs and how to link them to Python functions. This will allow you to generate dynamic content based on user requests. The next step is to learn about static files and templates. In this section, you will learn how to make and manage HTML templates that are compatible with Python and display information in an easy-to-understand way.

Interactive apps rely on the ability to handle file uploads and form submissions. The course will teach you how to take user input, process it, and react correctly; it will also teach you how to secure and validate data so that your application can withstand malicious input. Another important subject that we will learn is database integration. Flask SQL-Alchemy provides simple yet powerful tools for interacting with databases, allowing you to effectively store, retrieve, change, and delete data.

You will be exposed to a few of the most popular extensions that improve Flask's capabilities without cluttering your codebase, and you will learn how to use them to add more functionality to your Flask apps. Last but not least, you'll find out about different deployment tactics and platforms that can host your Flask app, allowing it to be accessible to people all over the globe.

By the end of this chapter, you will have learned all you need to know about Flask to create, maintain, and launch a fully-featured online app. This will lay the groundwork for future, more complex Flask features and bigger applications.

Flask Basics

What is Flask?

Developed by Armin Ronacher and released in 2010, Flask is based on the Werkzeug WSGI toolkit and Jinja2 template engine. Flask is a lightweight and flexible web framework for Python that is particularly well-suited for small to medium-sized applications and for developers who want fine-grained control over their components. Flask comes with minimal built-in features, which makes it simple and extensible, and a good choice for developers who prefer to build their applications from the ground up. It adheres to the principles of simplicity and fine control; it provides the tools needed to get a web application up and running with minimal setup, but also supports extensions to add additional functionality, such as object-relational mappers, form validation, and upload handling.

Core Features of Flask

Simplicity

Flask is considered more Pythonic than the Django web framework because it is minimalistic, and easy to learn. With Flask, you can have a simple web application running with just a few lines of code.

Flexibility

Flask lets you decide how you want to implement things. It allows you to use the tools you prefer to solve various problems like database interaction, URL routing, and template rendering.

Development Server and Debugger

Flask includes a built-in development server and debugger. The server lets you test your applications locally and reloads them automatically whenever it detects a change in the code. The debugger provides useful error messages and stack traces when something goes wrong.

Unicode Based

Flask supports Unicode out of the box, facilitating the use of non-ASCII characters in your applications, which is essential for international applications.

Documentation

Flask is well-documented with lots of available resources and a large community behind it. The official documentation is thorough and provides a good starting point for both beginners and experienced developers.

Up and Running with Flask

To get started with Flask, you'll need Python installed on your computer. Flask is compatible with Python 3.6 and newer. Given below is how you can set up a basic Flask application:

Install Flask using pip:

```
pip install Flask
```

Once Flask is installed, you can create a simple "Hello, World!" application:

```
from flask import Flask
```

```
app = Flask(__name__)


@app.route('/')
def hello_world():
 return 'Hello, World!'


if __name__ == '__main__':
 app.run(debug=True)
```

Given below is what each part of the code does:

- **from flask import Flask** imports the Flask class.

- **app = Flask(__name__)** creates an instance of the Flask class.

- **@app.route('/')** is a decorator that tells Flask what URL should trigger the function.

- **def hello_world():** defines the function that is called at the URL.

- **return 'Hello, World!'** is the response from the URL.

- **app.run(debug=True)** runs the app on a local development server, and the **debug=True** argument allows possible Python errors to appear on the web page.

Routing

Routing in Flask is handled with the **app.route** decorator. This decorator binds a function to a URL. Given below is an example of routing:

```
@app.route('/greet')
def greet():
 return 'Hello from Flask!'
```

You can also make parts of the URL dynamic and attach multiple rules to a function:

```
@app.route('/post/<int:post_id>')

def show_post(post_id):

  return 'Post %d' % post_id
```

In this case, **<int:post_id>** specifies that **post_id** should be an integer.

Templates

Flask uses Jinja2 as its template engine. A template is a file that contains static data as well as placeholders for dynamic data. A Flask route can render a template and return it to the client. Following is an example of how to render templates:

- First, create a directory named **templates** in your main application directory.

- Inside this directory, create an HTML file named **index.html**.

- Add the following content to **index.html**.

```
<h1>Hello {{ name }}!</h1>
```

- Render the Template

```
from flask import render_template


@app.route('/hello/<name>')

def hello(name=None):

  return render_template('index.html', name=name)
```

The **render_template** function takes the name of a template file and a variable list of template arguments and returns the same template, but with all placeholders in the template replaced with actual values.

Flask applications are easy to debug with the built-in development server. When you run the application with **app.run(debug=True)**, Flask provides an interactive debugger in the browser if your app encounters errors. Flask gives you everything you need to build APIs, web apps, or even learn backend development with little preparation and setup.

Setting up Flask Environment

In order to get your web app development started properly, you need to set up a Flask environment. This comprises a few steps. In this configuration, we will concentrate on project organization, dependency management, and critical service configuration.

Organizing your Project

A well-organized project structure is crucial for maintaining the codebase as the application grows. Following is a typical structure for a Flask project:

/app: This directory will contain your application code.

- **__init__.py**: Initializes your Flask app and brings together other components.

- **views.py**: Contains routes and views for your application.

- **models.py**: Contains the database models.

- **/static**: This directory holds static files like JavaScript, CSS, and images.

- **/templates**: Contains the Jinja2 templates.

/venv: Directory for the virtual environment (already set up as previously learned).

- **requirements.txt**: A file that lists all of your application's dependencies.

- **config.py**: Contains configuration variables and settings.

- **run.py**: The entry point for running your application.

Setting up Flask

Install Flask

Begin by ensuring Flask is installed in your Python environment. As learned previously, you can install Flask using pip:

```
pip install Flask
```

Create Flask Application

In the **__init__.py** file, set up your Flask application:

```
from flask import Flask
```

```
app = Flask(__name__)
```

```
from app import views
```

This script initializes the Flask application object as **app**. The app will import the **views** from your application which you will define in **views.py**.

Create Simple View

In **views.py**, define a simple route:

```
from app import app
```

```
@app.route('/')
def index():
 return "Hello Flask!"
```

Managing Dependencies with Pip

To handle project dependencies more efficiently, you should maintain a **requirements.txt** file. Whenever you install a new package, update this file:

```
pip freeze > requirements.txt
```

This file allows anyone who is setting up the project to easily install all required dependencies using:

```
pip install -r requirements.txt
```

Configuring Flask App

Configuration settings help you manage different environments (development, testing, production) more effectively.

Create Configuration File

Set up a **config.py** that stores configuration settings. This can include database URLs, secret keys, API keys, and other environmental settings:

```python
import os


class Config(object):
  SECRET_KEY = os.environ.get('SECRET_KEY') or 'you-will-never-guess'

  DEBUG = False

  TESTING = False


class ProductionConfig(Config):
  DATABASE_URI = 'mysql://user@localhost/foo'


class DevelopmentConfig(Config):
  DEBUG = True

  DATABASE_URI = 'sqlite:///development.db'


class TestingConfig(Config):
  TESTING = True

  DATABASE_URI = 'sqlite:///testing.db'
```

Load Configuration

In your **__init__.py**, configure your app to use these settings based on the current environment:

```
app.config.from_object('config.DevelopmentConfig')
```

Running the Flask Application

To run the Flask application, you can use the Flask command line or create a script:

Flask Command Line

Set environment variables to tell Flask how to import your app, then run it:

```
export FLASK_APP=run.py

export FLASK_ENV=development

flask run
```

Using a Script

Create a **run.py** at the root of your project:

```
from app import app


if __name__ == '__main__':
  app.run(debug=True)
```

You can then run your application by executing:

```
python run.py
```

By keeping the project organized, managing dependencies carefully, and utilizing configurations effectively, you can ensure that your development process is smooth and that your application is ready to handle different running environments.

Routing and Views

Now we'll get into one of the most fundamental parts of every web app: views and routing. When a user visits a certain URL in Flask, the routing feature determines what the app should display. You can respond to these requests by writing functions called views.

Defining Routes

In Flask, a route is the URL path to a particular function in your Python code, known as a 'view'. When Flask receives a request from a client (like a web browser), it matches the URL to a pre-defined route and then executes the associated view function, which generates the response.

Following is an example to define a basic route:

```python
from flask import Flask
app = Flask(__name__)


@app.route('/')
def home():
  return "Welcome to the Homepage!"
```

In this code, **@app.route('/')** is a decorator that tells Flask what URL should trigger the function that follows it. In this case, the **home** function is linked to the root URL of the website.

Dynamic Routes

Often, you'll need your application to handle dynamic content that changes based on the URL. For example, you might want to display information about a user or a specific product identified by an ID in the URL.

Following is how you can define dynamic routes in Flask:

```python
@app.route('/user/<username>')
def show_user_profile(username):
  # show the user profile for that user
  return f'User {username}'


@app.route('/post/<int:post_id>')
def show_post(post_id):
```

```
# show the post with the given id, the id is an integer

return f'Post {post_id}'
```

In the above code snippet, **<username>** and **<int:post_id>** are variable parts of the URL. Flask will accept any values put in these parts of the URL when routing requests and pass them as keyword arguments to the associated view functions.

HTTP Methods

By default, Flask routes respond to GET requests. However, if you want to handle different HTTP methods like POST, PUT, or DELETE, you can specify this using the **methods** argument in the route definition.

```
@app.route('/login', methods=['GET', 'POST'])

def login():

  if request.method == 'POST':

  return do_the_login()

  else:

  return show_the_login_form()
```

This function will respond differently to GET and POST requests. **request.method** contains the type of HTTP request made, and your logic can vary accordingly.

Constructing URLs

To build URLs for a specific function, you can use the **url_for()** function. This function generates URLs using the function's name and arguments.

```
from flask import url_for

@app.route('/')

def index():

  return 'index'
```

```python
@app.route('/login')
def login():
  return 'login'


@app.route('/user/<username>')
def profile(username):
  return f'{username}\'s profile'


with app.test_request_context():
  print(url_for('index'))
  print(url_for('login'))
  print(url_for('login', next='/'))
  print(url_for('profile', username='John Doe'))
```

url_for('index') will generate the URL to the **index** view. This is especially useful for avoiding hard-coding URLs in your templates and scripts, making your application easier to maintain.

Error Handling

Handling errors properly is crucial for a good user experience. Flask allows you to easily define custom error pages for different error types.

```python
@app.errorhandler(404)
def page_not_found(error):
  return "This page does not exist.", 404


@app.errorhandler(500)
```

```
def internal_server_error(error):
 return "Internal server error.", 500
```

These handlers make it easy to return user-friendly error messages when things go wrong.

Combining Routes and Views Effectively

The power of Flask lies in its simplicity and flexibility in routing and view functions. Combining them effectively allows you to:

- Serve dynamic content that adapts to the data or user requests.

- Handle forms and user input safely and securely.

- Create RESTful interfaces that can interact with other services or front ends.

As you develop more complex applications, you may find the need to organize routes and views better. Flask supports blueprints for this purpose, which allow you to organize your application into components that can be easily reused or configured.

Templates and Static Files

Now that we've covered the basics of Flask views and routing, let's move on to managing templates and static files. If you want your web app to have a responsive and interesting user experience and serve dynamic content, you must have these components.

Understanding Templates

Templates in Flask are a powerful feature used to generate dynamic HTML content. Powered by the Jinja2 template engine, Flask allows you to create HTML templates with placeholders for dynamic content that your application can produce based on user interactions or other inputs.

Templates in Flask are usually HTML files with additional placeholders for dynamic content. These placeholders are specified using Jinja2's template syntax. For instance, you can pass variables from your Flask view function to a template and use these variables to populate fields within the HTML.

Given below is how to set up and use templates:

- Create a templates folder in your project directory. Flask automatically looks for templates in a folder named templates.

- Inside the **templates** folder, create an HTML file, for example, **template.html**. Following is an example of what this file might look like:

```html
<!DOCTYPE html>
<html>
<head>
 <title>{{ title }}</title>
</head>
<body>
 <h1>Hello {{ name }}!</h1>
 {% if messages %}
 <ul>
 {% for message in messages %}
 <li>{{ message }}</li>
 {% endfor %}
 </ul>
 {% else %}
 <p>No messages.</p>
 {% endif %}
</body>
</html>
```

- In this template, **{{ title }}**, **{{ name }}**, and **{{ messages }}** are placeholders that will be filled with data passed from a Flask view.
- In your Flask view, use the **render_template()** function to serve this HTML file, passing variables as keyword arguments:

```
from flask import render_template
```

```
@app.route('/')

def index():

 return render_template('template.html', title='Home
Page', name='John Doe', messages=['Hello', 'Hi', 'Hey'])
```

This setup allows the server to render dynamic content based on the data it receives, making your application interactive and user-responsive.

Managing Static Files

Static files are the components of your website that don't change dynamically, such as JavaScript files, CSS stylesheets, and images. Managing these files efficiently is crucial for performance and maintainability.

Organizing Static Files

Create a **static** folder in your project directory. Flask automatically looks for static files in a folder named **static**. You should organize your files into subfolders like **css**, **js**, and **images** for better structure.

```
/YourApp

 /static

 /css

 style.css

 /js

 script.js

 /images

 logo.png
```

Serving Static Files

Flask provides a built-in way to reference static files in your templates. Use the **url_for()** function to generate URLs for static files:

```html
<link rel="stylesheet" type="text/css" href="{{
url_for('static', filename='css/style.css') }}">

<script src="{{ url_for('static',
filename='js/script.js') }}"></script>

<img src="{{ url_for('static',
filename='images/logo.png') }}" alt="Company Logo">
```

This method ensures that the correct paths are generated for your files, regardless of where your application is hosted. It also helps to avoid hardcoding paths, which can lead to errors and make your code harder to maintain.

While you do so, do follow the following best practices for templates and static files:

- Since static files don't change often, you should implement caching techniques to improve load times for repeat visitors. This can typically be configured at the web server level or through HTTP headers.

- For production, minimize CSS and JavaScript files to reduce load times and bandwidth usage.

- Use Jinja2's template inheritance feature to create a base "skeleton" template that contains all the common elements of your site (like header, footer, and navigation) and extend this base template in other templates. This reduces redundancy and helps manage changes more effectively.

```html
<!-- base.html -->

<html>

<head>

 <title>{% block title %}{% endblock %}</title>

</head>

<body>

 {% block body %}

 {% endblock %}

</body>
```

```
</html>
```

```
<!-- home.html -->
{% extends "base.html" %}
{% block title %}Home{% endblock %}
{% block body %}
<h1>Welcome to the Home Page</h1>
<p>Hello, {{ name }}!</p>
{% endblock %}
```

Make sure your Flask app keeps a clean, engaging UI and provides content dynamically by managing static files and templates efficiently. In addition to improving efficiency, these techniques also make your web app look more polished and professional, which in turn improves the user experience.

Form Handling and File Uploads

Handling Forms in Flask

Forms are essential for capturing user input. Flask can handle form data seamlessly using the **request** object. To demonstrate form handling, we'll use a simple contact form as an example.

Create HTML Form

In your **templates** directory, create a new file named **contact.html**. Following is a basic form for user input:

```
<form method="post" action="{{ url_for('handle_form')
}}">
  <label for="name">Name:</label>
  <input type="text" id="name" name="name"><br><br>
```

```html
<label for="email">Email:</label>

<input type="text" id="email" name="email"><br><br>

<input type="submit" value="Submit">

</form>
```

This form collects a user's name and email, which will be sent to a Flask route for processing.

Create Route to Display Form

In your Flask application, define a route to render this form:

```python
@app.route('/contact')

def contact():

  return render_template('contact.html')
```

Handling Form Data

When the form is submitted, the data needs to be captured and processed by another route. Given below is how you can handle the POST request:

```python
from flask import request, redirect, url_for


@app.route('/handle_form', methods=['POST'])

def handle_form():

 name = request.form['name']

 email = request.form['email']

 # Process or store the form data here

 return redirect(url_for('thank_you'))
```

This code extracts data from the form fields and then you can process it as needed (e.g., storing it in a database or sending an email).

File Uploads

Handling file uploads allows users to send files through forms, which can be particularly useful for applications that require user documents, images, or other media.

Modifying HTML Form for File Uploads

To allow file uploads, modify your form to include an **enctype** attribute and a file input field:

```html
<form method="post" action="{{
url_for('handle_file_upload') }}"
enctype="multipart/form-data">
  <label for="uploaded_file">Upload file:</label>
  <input type="file" id="uploaded_file" name="file">
  <input type="submit" value="Upload">
</form>
```

The **enctype="multipart/form-data"** attribute is essential for telling the browser how to properly package the file being uploaded.

Handling File Uploads in Flask

Create a route to handle the file upload. You'll need to ensure the file is safe to save and then process it accordingly.

```python
import os

from werkzeug.utils import secure_filename


@app.route('/handle_file_upload', methods=['POST'])
def handle_file_upload():
 file = request.files['file']
 if file and allowed_file(file.filename):
 filename = secure_filename(file.filename)
```

```
file.save(os.path.join(app.config['UPLOAD_FOLDER'],
filename))

 return redirect(url_for('uploaded_file',
filename=filename))

 return 'File upload unsuccessful'
```

In the above code snippet, **secure_filename** ensures that the filename is safe from harmful characters, and **allowed_file** checks the file extension against a set of allowed extensions (a function you would define to limit uploads to safe file types).

While working around form handling and uploads, always validate and sanitize incoming data to prevent common vulnerabilities such as SQL injection, cross-site scripting (XSS), and others. For forms, Flask-WTF can be used to simplify form creation and handle validations. Set a maximum file size for uploads. Flask allows configuring **MAX_CONTENT_LENGTH** to reject incoming requests with too much data.

Database Integration Basics

Any Flask-based dynamic web app that needs persistent data storage must have database integration. Flask is built to be readily integrated with a range of database technologies, including SQL and NoSQL choices, however it does not have an ORM or database abstraction layer by default. In this section, we'll look at how to connect a SQL database to a Flask project using SQLAlchemy, a well-known object relational mapping (ORM) for Python.

Setting up SQLAlchemy with Flask

SQLAlchemy provides a powerful and flexible way to communicate with databases through Pythonic models and queries. Flask-SQLAlchemy is an extension that adds SQLAlchemy support to your Flask application in a way that is more Flask-friendly.

Install Flask-SQLAlchemy

First, you'll need to add Flask-SQLAlchemy to your environment:

```
pip install flask_sqlalchemy
```

Configure Application

Add database configuration settings to your Flask application:

```python
from flask import Flask

from flask_sqlalchemy import SQLAlchemy


app = Flask(__name__)

app.config['SQLALCHEMY_DATABASE_URI'] =
'sqlite:///yourdatabase.db'

app.config['SQLALCHEMY_TRACK_MODIFICATIONS'] = False

db = SQLAlchemy(app)
```

In the above code snippet, **SQLALCHEMY_DATABASE_URI** is used to define the path to your database file, specifying the database type and location. **SQLALCHEMY_TRACK_MODIFICATIONS** is set to **False** to disable signal handling, which helps to save resources.

Defining Models

Models in SQLAlchemy are used to define the structure of your database tables in Python code. They are classes that define the fields in the table and can also include methods to interact with the data.

```python
class User(db.Model):
  id = db.Column(db.Integer, primary_key=True)
  username = db.Column(db.String(80), unique=True,
nullable=False)
  email = db.Column(db.String(120), unique=True,
nullable=False)


  def __repr__(self):
  return '<User %r>' % self.username
```

In the above code snippet, **User** is a model with **id**, **username**, and **email** fields. The **id** field is defined as the primary key.

Creating Database

With your models defined, you can create your database tables:

```
db.create_all()
```

This command looks at all the classes that inherit from **db.Model** and creates tables for them if the tables do not already exist.

Interacting with Database

SQLAlchemy allows you to interact with the database using Python code rather than writing SQL queries, which helps maintain the integrity and security of the data.

Inserting Data

```
new_user = User(username='johndoe',
email='johndoe@gitforgits.com')

db.session.add(new_user)

db.session.commit()
```

This snippet creates a new instance of the **User** model and adds it to the database session. **db.session.commit()** commits all pending transactions to the database.

Querying Data

```
user = User.query.filter_by(username='johndoe').first()

print(user.email)
```

This query retrieves the first user with the username 'johndoe' from the database and prints their email.

Updating Data

```
user = User.query.filter_by(username='johndoe').first()

user.email = 'newemail@gitforgits.com'
```

```
db.session.commit()
```

In the above code snippet, the email of the user is updated, and the changes are committed to the database.

Deleting Data

```
user = User.query.get(1) # Assumes '1' is the id of the
user

db.session.delete(user)

db.session.commit()
```

This code snippet retrieves a user by their ID and then deletes that user from the database.

Handling Relationships

SQLAlchemy can also handle relationships between tables:

```
class Post(db.Model):
 id = db.Column(db.Integer, primary_key=True)
 title = db.Column(db.String(100), nullable=False)
 content = db.Column(db.Text, nullable=False)
 user_id = db.Column(db.Integer,
db.ForeignKey('user.id'), nullable=False)
 user = db.relationship('User',
backref=db.backref('posts', lazy=True))
```

In the above,, the **user** relationship allows us to easily access all posts created by a user. The **backref** argument in the **db.relationship()** method creates a reverse relationship where you can access the posts from the user object.

Retrieving Related Data

To retrieve data that utilizes these relationships, you can do the following:

```
user = User.query.get(1) # Get the user with id=1

posts = user.posts # Access all posts made by this user

for post in posts:

 print(post.title)
```

This code demonstrates how to fetch a user by their ID and then access all posts related to that user through the **posts** attribute. This attribute is provided by the **backref='posts'** in the relationship defined in the **Post** model.

Leveraging Query Options

SQLAlchemy provides numerous options to optimize and customize queries, such as lazy loading, eager loading, and dynamic loading, which can help in managing database sessions and performance:

1. Lazy Loading: The default behavior where SQLAlchemy loads data as necessary in a separate query per access. Suitable for smaller databases or fewer relationships.

2. Eager Loading: Loads all data upfront using joins and subqueries. This is useful when you know you will need all the related data and want to minimize the number of queries made.

3. Dynamic Loading: Setup relationships as queries that are not loaded until specifically queried. This is useful for larger sets of related items.

Given below is how you can specify eager loading to optimize data retrieval:

```
from sqlalchemy.orm import joinedload


user =
User.query.options(joinedload(User.posts)).filter_by(user
name='johndoe').first()

for post in user.posts:

 print(post.title)
```

This approach configures SQLAlchemy to load all related **Post** objects at the same time as the **User** object using a single query, which can significantly improve performance by reducing the number of database hits.

Whether you're dealing with basic operations or advanced transactions, SQLAlchemy has you covered with the tools you need to securely and efficiently access your database. Thus, this database connectivity does double duty: it improves functionality and guarantees that your Flask apps may scale up or down without a hitch.

Introduction to Flask Extensions

You may discover that the built-in features of Flask aren't enough for your application's demands as it becomes more complicated and functional. The use of Flask extensions becomes relevant in this context. From the object relationship management (ORM) capabilities with SQLAlchemy that we covered previously to user authentication, migration management, and many more, Flask's extensive ecosystem of extensions may enhance your applications.

Understanding Flask Extensions

Flask extensions are packages or modules that extend the functionality of Flask. They are developed to integrate seamlessly with Flask apps, adhering to the framework's patterns and conventions. These extensions often simplify the use of other libraries within Flask, handle boilerplate code, and add new capabilities.

Let us explore some commonly used Flask extensions that address various needs in web application development:

Flask-WTF

Simplifies form handling, integrating WTForms to manage web forms seamlessly. It includes CSRF protection and validators to ensure that the data submitted by users is safe and valid.

```
from flask_wtf import FlaskForm

from wtforms import StringField, PasswordField,
SubmitField

from wtforms.validators import InputRequired, Length,
Email


class LoginForm(FlaskForm):

 username = StringField('Username',
validators=[InputRequired(), Length(min=4, max=15)])
```

```python
    password = PasswordField('Password',
validators=[InputRequired(), Length(min=8, max=80)])

    submit = SubmitField('Login')
```

Flask-SQLAlchemy

Provides an ORM layer for handling database operations in Flask using SQLAlchemy. It simplifies database manipulation, making it more intuitive and Pythonic.

```python
from flask_sqlalchemy import SQLAlchemy


db = SQLAlchemy(app)
```

Flask-Migrate

Handles SQLAlchemy database migrations for Flask applications. It leverages Alembic and allows you to track database schema changes through migrations, which can be shared and applied to different instances of the application.

```python
from flask_migrate import Migrate


migrate = Migrate(app, db)
```

Flask-Login

Provides user session management. It handles the common tasks of logging in, logging out, and remembering users' sessions over extended periods.

```python
from flask_login import LoginManager, UserMixin,
login_user, logout_user, current_user


login_manager = LoginManager(app)

login_manager.login_view = 'login'
```

Flask-Mail

Adds SMTP email sending capabilities to your Flask applications, which is handy for features like user confirmation emails, password resets, and notifications.

```
from flask_mail import Mail, Message


mail = Mail(app)
```

Flask-RESTful

Encourages best practices with REST and simplifies the creation of REST APIs. It provides a resource-based approach to building HTTP APIs and handles request parsing and output formatting.

```
from flask_restful import Api, Resource


api = Api(app)


class HelloWorld(Resource):
 def get(self):
 return {'hello': 'world'}


api.add_resource(HelloWorld, '/')
```

Using Flask Extensions

To use a Flask extension, you generally follow these steps:

Install the Extension

Use pip to install the extension.

```
pip install flask-wtf
```

Import and Initialize

Import the extension and initialize it with your Flask app.

```
from flask_wtf import CSRFProtect
```

```
app = Flask(__name__)
```

```
csrf = CSRFProtect(app)
```

Configure

Many extensions require specific configuration options, which are usually set directly on the Flask app's **config** dictionary.

```
app.config['SECRET_KEY'] = 'your_secret_key'
```

```
app.config['SQLALCHEMY_DATABASE_URI'] =
'sqlite:///db.sqlite'
```

Then, you simply incorporate the extension's functionality in your application logic. Extensions enhance Flask's capabilities and allow for more structured code and feature-rich applications. As you continue to expand your Flask knowledge and toolset, exploring different extensions can significantly impact how you approach building applications, allowing you to focus on unique business logic rather than common backend functionalities.

Deploying Flask Application

It is essential to deploy your Flask application so that it can be accessed by users on the internet after you have built it and integrated numerous capabilities through extensions. Getting a Flask project ready for production, selecting a hosting provider, and configuring a web server and WSGI application server are all part of the deployment process.

Preparing Flask Application for Deployment

Switch to Production Database

If you've been using SQLite or another development-focused database, consider migrating to a production-ready database like PostgreSQL, MySQL, or another robust database management system suited for handling concurrent access and large data volumes.

Use Environment Variables for Configuration

Store sensitive information such as database URIs, secret keys, and third-party API credentials in environment variables instead of hard-coding them into your application's source code. This enhances security and flexibility in different environments.

Remove Debug Mode

Ensure that the debug mode is turned off in your Flask application. Leaving debug mode on in a production environment can expose sensitive information and vulnerabilities.

```
app.config['DEBUG'] = False
```

Choosing Hosting Service

Several options are available for hosting Flask applications, ranging from traditional shared hosts to more modern application platforms:

1. Heroku: A popular platform-as-a-service (PaaS) that simplifies deploying, managing, and scaling web applications. Heroku can run Flask applications natively and handles much of the configuration automatically.

2. DigitalOcean, AWS, and Google Cloud: These infrastructure-as-a-service (IaaS) providers offer more control over the server and environment. They require a bit more setup but provide the flexibility to configure the system to your specific needs.

3. PythonAnywhere: An online IDE and hosting service that is particularly friendly to Python and Flask applications.

Setting up Web Server and WSGI Application Server

To serve your Flask application to visitors, you need a web server and a WSGI (Web Server Gateway Interface) application server. The web server handles HTTP requests and serves static files, while the WSGI server runs your Python code.

- Gunicorn: A popular WSGI server for Unix-based systems. It's lightweight, supports multiple worker processes, and is easy to configure with Flask.

- Nginx: A robust, high-performance web server that can act as a reverse proxy and load balancer. It's typically used in conjunction with Gunicorn to serve static files and handle client connections.

Using Heroku

Deploying a Flask application to Heroku involves the following steps:

Prepare Application

- Ensure your application structure is correct, and all dependencies are listed in **requirements.txt**.

- Create a **Procfile**, which tells Heroku how to run your application:

```
web: gunicorn app:app
```

In this **Procfile**, **web** indicates that this process type is web-accessible, and **gunicorn app:app** tells Heroku to use Gunicorn to run the application.

Set up Git Repository

If you haven't already, initialize a Git repository in your project folder and commit your files.

```
git init

git add .

git commit -m "Initial commit"
```

Create Heroku App

- Install the Heroku CLI and log in to your Heroku account. Create a new app:

```
heroku create your-app-name
```

Deploy Your application by pushing your code to Heroku:

```
git push heroku master
```

- Then, set environment variables on Heroku.

```
heroku config:set FLASK_APP=run.py

heroku config:set SECRET_KEY='your_secret_key'
```

Verify Deployment

- Open your application in a web browser using the URL provided by Heroku or by running:

```
heroku open
```

There are a number of important things to do before deploying a Flask application, such as getting the app ready for production, choosing a good hosting provider, and setting up a web server and WSGI application server. If you follow these steps, your Flask application will be deployed safely and effectively, ready to handle real-world traffic and interactions.

Summary

This chapter covered the groundwork for building and releasing a Flask-based web app. In our first step into Flask, we covered the fundamentals, such as how to create a basic Flask environment and construct web applications with minimal code but enough power. Once we mastered routing, we moved on to views, which are fundamental for specifying how an application responds to user input.

Additionally, we learned the Flask framework's handling of static files and templates. We were able to seamlessly integrate Python logic into our web pages with the use of templates, which enabled us to dynamically generate HTML content using the Jinja2 template engine. The application's functionality and aesthetics are enhanced by static files, which must be handled properly in order to manage JavaScript, CSS, and picture files. Securely capturing and processing user inputs is a crucial feature for interactive websites, and this chapter taught us how to do just that through learning form handling and file uploads. The Flask-SQLAlchemy package taught us how to connect to a database and how to efficiently execute CRUD (Create, Read, Update, and Delete) activities.

We concluded by looking into a number of Flask extensions that provided additional features, such as authentication for users, email processing, and advanced object relationship management capabilities. A complete practical on launching a Flask app served as the chapter's capstone. To make sure the software was ready for production, we tested several deployment methods and created environments. From basic routing to advanced database interactions and deployment tactics, we learned it all in this chapter as we progressively built a Flask web application from the ground up.

CHAPTER 3: ADVANCED FLASK DEVELOPMENT

Introduction

This chapter explores the more advanced features of Flask, with an emphasis on patterns and best practices for securing and scaling Flask applications. New problems arise when Flask projects expand in size and complexity, necessitating more sophisticated approaches and methods. If you're looking to maximize performance, reliability, security, and the structure of larger applications, this chapter has you covered.

First, we'll look at how to use Flask Blueprints to organize bigger applications. The use of blueprints facilitates the management and scalability of huge projects by breaking them down into smaller, reusable components. The Flask Application Factory pattern is next, and it's a significant way to manage various application settings and environments because it's versatile and adjustable when it comes to creating Flask instances.

Following an introduction to RESTful services, this chapter delves into how to use Flask-RESTful, an extension that streamlines the process of developing REST APIs. How to build and deploy RESTful APIs that can scale is the topic of this section.

Protecting web applications requires strong authentication and permission of users. Here, you will learn about several approaches to authentication, session management, and permission-based access control in applications.

Application dependability and traceability are also significantly affected by error management and logging. We go over some methods for handling and documenting exceptions and errors, as well as some approaches to debugging and troubleshooting.

Next, we'll take a look at performance optimization strategies, with an emphasis on how to make Flask applications faster and more efficient. Several techniques for improving your Flask apps will be covered, including how to communicate with databases and handle requests.

Lastly, Flask application integration with Docker demonstrates how to containerize Flask apps, which streamlines deployment and offers predictable settings for QA, production, and development. If you want to make your Flask apps more portable and easier to deploy, this section will show you how to create Docker containers that encapsulate your environment and dependencies.

Structuring Larger Applications with Flask Blueprints

Managing the entire application within a single module or script becomes impractical when Flask applications expand in complexity and size. This is where the Flask Blueprints feature becomes useful. Blueprints allow you to break down your Flask app into smaller, reusable parts, which could individually run their own app. Large applications can be made more manageable and modular with their support.

What are Flask Blueprints?

Blueprints can be thought of as mini-applications that do not actually run by themselves but are registered with the main Flask application at runtime. They are a means to organize your project by feature or functionality and can be reused across multiple projects.

Blueprints facilitate the separation of concerns by allowing you to isolate features and components into distinct parts of the application, each with its own static files, templates, views, forms, and other elements. For example, you might have one blueprint for authentication, another for the blog backend, and another for the admin interface.

Creating and Registering Blueprints

Here's how to define and register a Blueprint:

Define Blueprint

You start by importing the **Blueprint** class and then creating an instance of it. The **Blueprint** constructor takes two required arguments: the blueprint name and the module or package where the blueprint is located.

```
from flask import Blueprint
```

```
auth = Blueprint('auth', __name__,
template_folder='templates')
```

In the above code snippet, **auth** is the name of the blueprint, and **__name__** ensures that the blueprint knows where it's defined. The **template_folder** argument is optional and can be used to specify where the templates for this blueprint are stored.

Register Blueprint

After defining a blueprint, you must register it with the application to make use of it. This is typically done in your application factory.

```
from flask import Flask
```

```
from yourapplication.auth import auth
```

```
app = Flask(__name__)

app.register_blueprint(auth, url_prefix='/auth')
```

The **url_prefix** parameter is optional but useful for adding a prefix to all routes registered with the blueprint. In this case, all routes defined in the **auth** blueprint will be prefixed with **/auth**.

Structuring Views in Blueprints

After setting up your blueprint, you can start adding routes and views to it. Given below is how you can add a view to the **auth** blueprint.

```
# in yourapplication/auth/views.py


from . import auth


@auth.route('/login', methods=['GET', 'POST'])
def login():
 return "Login Here"
```

Using Blueprints

When your application grows, you might have several distinct functionalities, each potentially deserving its own blueprint. Following is how you might structure a larger application.

```
/yourapplication
 /auth
 __init__.py
 views.py
 models.py
```

```
/blog

__init__.py

views.py

models.py

/admin

__init__.py

views.py

/static

/templates

__init__.py

config.py

run.py
```

In this structure:

- Each feature (auth, blog, admin) is separated into its own directory, potentially with its own templates and static files.

- The root of each feature directory contains an **__init__.py** where the blueprint is defined and configured.

Blueprints enhance the scalability of Flask applications by allowing developers to modularize features into separate components, making the codebase easier to manage and extend. This modular architecture enables better collaboration across large teams by minimizing merge conflicts and ensuring that different parts of the application can evolve somewhat independently.

Flask Application Factory Pattern

Understanding Flask Application Factory Pattern

The Flask Application Factory pattern is a design choice that significantly enhances the scalability and flexibility of Flask applications, especially as they grow larger and more complex. The Application Factory pattern involves defining a function that creates and returns a Flask application instance. The main advantage of this pattern is that it allows the configuration, extensions, blueprints, and other components to be dynamically altered based on the runtime environment or other external factors. This is achieved without the need to change the application's source code, enhancing maintainability and deployment flexibility.

Implementing Application Factory Pattern

Following is a step-by-step procedure on implementing the Flask Application Factory pattern:

Create Factory Function

The factory function typically resides in the main package of your application. It configures and returns the Flask application object.

```
from flask import Flask
from config import Config


def create_app(config_class=Config):
  app = Flask(__name__)
  app.config.from_object(config_class)


  return app
```

In the above sample program, **create_app** takes a configuration class as an argument, which it uses to configure the Flask app instance. The default **config_class** is **Config**, which could be a Python class that contains configuration variables.

Organize Configuration Settings

Configuration settings can be organized into different classes in a separate **config.py** file. Each class can correspond to a different deployment environment.

```
class Config:
  DEBUG = False
  TESTING = False
```

```
    DATABASE_URI = 'sqlite:///example.db'


class DevelopmentConfig(Config):
  DEBUG = True


class TestingConfig(Config):
  TESTING = True
  DATABASE_URI = 'sqlite:///test.db'


class ProductionConfig(Config):
  DATABASE_URI = 'mysql://user@localhost/foo'
```

This setup allows you to easily switch configurations by passing different configuration classes to the **create_app** function.

Register Blueprints and Extensions

Inside the factory function, after configuring the app, register any extensions and blueprints. This step ensures that these components are tied specifically to an instance of the application.

```
from .extensions import db, migrate
from .routes import main, admin


def create_app(config_class=Config):
  app = Flask(__name__)
  app.config.from_object(config_class)


  db.init_app(app)
```

```
migrate.init_app(app, db)


app.register_blueprint(main)

app.register_blueprint(admin)


return app
```

In the above code snippet, **db** and **migrate** are Flask extensions, and **main** and **admin** are blueprints.

In practice, you would use the factory pattern when running locally:

```
export FLASK_APP=myapp:create_app('DevelopmentConfig')
flask run
```

And, in production:

```
export FLASK_APP=myapp:create_app('ProductionConfig')
```

This method allows the environment variable **FLASK_APP** to specify not just the application to run but also how it should be configured. The factory function **create_app** is powerful and versatile, allowing you to tailor the Flask instance to the needs of each specific environment or situation.

Implementing RESTful Services with Flask-RESTful

RESTful services are a way of designing web applications to interact via HTTP in a manner consistent with the core protocols of the web. REST (Representational State Transfer) principles allow for scalable and simple interactions by using standard HTTP methods like GET, POST, PUT, DELETE, etc., to perform actions. These principles help in creating services that are stateless and can be easily consumed by different clients including browsers, mobile apps, and other web services.

Introduction to Flask-RESTful

Flask-RESTful is an extension for Flask that adds support for quickly building REST APIs. It is a lightweight abstraction that works on top of Flask's usual routing mechanisms. Flask-RESTful simplifies API creation through its resource-based approach, where each resource corresponds to a specific entity and can be accessed or manipulated using standard HTTP methods.

Functioning of Flask-RESTful

Flask-RESTful provides a **Resource** class which you can subclass to define the logic for handling various HTTP methods. The association between the HTTP methods and the resource methods is direct; for instance, a GET request to a resource is handled by the **get()** method of that resource, a POST request by the **post()** method, and so forth. This resource is then registered with the API object, linking it with a specific endpoint.

Creation of REST API using Flask-RESTful

To illustrate creating a REST API with Flask-RESTful, let's build a simple API for managing "items" in a store.

- Install Flask-RESTful:
  - Start by installing the Flask-RESTful extension:

```
pip install flask-restful
```

- Set up the Flask Application:
  - Create a new Flask application and import the Flask-RESTful extension:

```
from flask import Flask
from flask_restful import Api, Resource


app = Flask(__name__)
api = Api(app)
```

- Define Resource Classes:
  - Define a resource class for your entity. In this case, create an **Item** resource with methods to handle different HTTP methods:

```python
class Item(Resource):
 def get(self, name):
 return {'item': name}


 def post(self, name):
 return {'item': name}, 201


 def delete(self, name):
 return {'message': f'Item {name} deleted'}


class ItemList(Resource):
 def get(self):
 return {'items': ['Item1', 'Item2']}
```

- o Each method corresponds to a RESTful HTTP method. For instance, **get** returns an item, **post** creates an item, and **delete** removes an item.
- Add Resources to the API:
  - o Register the resource classes with specific routes:

```python
api.add_resource(Item, '/item/<string:name>')
api.add_resource(ItemList, '/items')
```

- o The **add_resource** method links the **Item** class to the route **/item/<string:name>**, where **<string:name>** is a variable part of the URL.
- Run the Flask Application:

- Set the Flask application to run with debugging enabled. This is typically done in a conditional block to prevent it from running when the script is imported as a module:

```
if __name__ == '__main__':
 app.run(debug=True)
```

- This starts a local development server for the Flask application.

Testing the API

Once your Flask application is running, you can test the API endpoints using a tool like Postman or curl. For example, to get the item list, you might send a GET request to **http://localhost:5000/items**, or to add an item, send a POST request to **http://localhost:5000/item/apple**.

By defining these resources and mapping them to routes, you can create an intuitive and scalable API that adheres to REST principles. This makes Flask-RESTful a valuable tool for developers looking to build efficient and effective REST APIs in Python using Flask.

User Authentication and Authorization

To guarantee that only authorized users can access designated resources or carry out specified actions according to their rights, user authentication and authorization are essential components of web application security. While permission determines what an authenticated user can do, authentication verifies the user's identity.

Importance of Authentication, Authorization and Session Management

Authentication

- Authentication confirms that users are who they claim to be.
- It ensures that users can only access resources after they have successfully authenticated, protecting sensitive information from unauthorized access.

Authorization

- After authentication, authorization checks ensure that a user has the correct permissions to access a resource or execute a specific operation.

- By implementing detailed permission levels, applications can minimize the risk of accidental or malicious misuse of the system.

Session Management

- Web applications often need to maintain a user's state (or session) between different requests. Proper session management ensures that this state is preserved securely.

Implementing Authentication in Flask

Flask does not have built-in authentication mechanisms, but it can be easily implemented with extensions such as Flask-Login for handling user sessions.

Installing Flask-Login

```
pip install flask-login
```

Configuring Flask-Login

Flask-Login provides user session management for Flask. It handles the common tasks of logging in, logging out, and remembering users' sessions.

```
from flask_login import LoginManager, UserMixin,
login_user, logout_user, login_required


app = Flask(__name__)

app.secret_key = 'your_secret_key' # Used to secure the
sessions


login_manager = LoginManager()

login_manager.init_app(app)

login_manager.login_view = 'login'
```

User Loader Function

The **login_manager** requires a user loader function that loads a user from a given ID.

```
@login_manager.user_loader
def load_user(user_id):
  return User.query.get(int(user_id))
```

Defining User Model

The user model should inherit from **UserMixin**, which adds default implementations for several properties and methods used by Flask-Login.

```
from flask_sqlalchemy import SQLAlchemy

from flask_login import UserMixin


db = SQLAlchemy(app)


class User(db.Model, UserMixin):
  id = db.Column(db.Integer, primary_key=True)
  username = db.Column(db.String(25), unique=True,
nullable=False)
  password = db.Column(db.String(80), nullable=False)
```

Creating Authentication Routes

Implement routes for login and logout functionalities.

```
@app.route('/login', methods=['GET', 'POST'])
def login():
  if request.method == 'POST':
  username = request.form['username']
  password = request.form['password']
```

```python
    user = User.query.filter_by(username=username).first()
    if user and user.password == password: # Simple password
check
        login_user(user)
        return redirect(url_for('dashboard'))
    else:
        return 'Invalid username or password'
    return render_template('login.html')


@app.route('/logout')
@login_required
def logout():
    logout_user()
    return redirect(url_for('login'))


@app.route('/dashboard')
@login_required
def dashboard():
    return 'Welcome to your Dashboard!'
```

Implementing Authorization

Authorization can be managed by extending the user model or using Flask extensions to handle roles and permissions.

Role-Based Access Control (RBAC)

You might define roles and permissions directly in your database model.

```python
class Role(db.Model):
  id = db.Column(db.Integer, primary_key=True)
  name = db.Column(db.String(50), unique=True)


class UserRole(db.Model):
  user_id = db.Column(db.Integer,
db.ForeignKey('user.id'), primary_key=True)

  role_id = db.Column(db.Integer,
db.ForeignKey('role.id'), primary_key=True)
```

Checking Permissions

Decorators or helper functions can be used to check if a user has a specific role or permission before allowing access to a route.

```python
def requires_roles(*roles):
  def wrapper(f):
  @wraps(f)
  def wrapped(*args, **kwargs):
  if not current_user.has_role(roles):
  return 'Unauthorized', 403
  return f(*args, **kwargs)
  return wrapped
  return wrapper


@app.route('/admin')
@login_required
```

```
@requires_roles('admin')

def admin():

 return 'Admin Page'
```

Flask apps can protect user information and make sure people can only access what they are authorized to by incorporating these authentication and authorization systems. Additionally, this configuration aids in keeping a safe and user-specific interaction environment, which in turn protects the program from illegal access.

Error Handling and Logging

In order to fix problems, make error messages more helpful to users, and maintain track of program activities for analysis, error handling and logging are mandatory. Flask allows for efficient configuration of error handling and logging to control the catching of exceptions and the logging of information about the application's execution.

Error Handling in Flask

Flask provides built-in support for handling errors that occur within an application, including unhandled exceptions and HTTP errors. Given below is how to set up custom error handling in a Flask application.

Handling Application Errors

You can define custom error handlers in Flask using the **@app.errorhandler** decorator, which catches errors and exceptions thrown during execution.

```
@app.errorhandler(404)

def not_found_error(error):

 return render_template('404.html'), 404


@app.errorhandler(500)

def internal_error(error):
```

```
db.session.rollback() # assuming you are using
SQLAlchemy
```

```
return render_template('500.html'), 500
```

In this setup, **404** and **500** are the status codes for "Not Found" and "Internal Server Error," respectively. The functions return custom templates that inform the user about the error in a friendlier manner.

Handling Exceptions

Flask allows you to handle Python exceptions directly, giving you control over the response when something goes wrong in the application logic.

```
@app.errorhandler(Exception)
```

```
def handle_exception(e):
```

```
 # pass through HTTP errors
```

```
 if isinstance(e, HTTPException):
```

```
 return e
```

```
 # now you're handling non-HTTP exceptions only
```

```
 return render_template("error_generic.html", error=e),
500
```

Logging in Flask

Application monitoring and troubleshooting rely heavily on logging. To output messages to a file or the console, Flask employs Python's in-built logging module. To keep track of requests, failures, and operational data, set up logging in your Flask project as below:

```
import logging
```

```
from logging.handlers import RotatingFileHandler
```

```
if not app.debug:
```

```
file_handler =
RotatingFileHandler('instance/flask_app.log',
maxBytes=10240,

 backupCount=10)

 file_handler.setFormatter(logging.Formatter(

 '%(asctime)s %(levelname)s: %(message)s [in
%(pathname)s:%(lineno)d]'

 ))

 app.logger.addHandler(file_handler)

 app.logger.setLevel(logging.INFO)

 app.logger.info('Flask application startup')
```

This configuration sets up a rotating log handler, which means the log file will automatically be "rotated" (i.e., a new file started) when the current file reaches a certain size. It also formats the log messages to include timestamps, the severity level of the events, and the source of the log entry.

Using Logging for Request Data

To debug issues related to specific requests, you can log data about each request and response. Flask can automatically log this information if configured properly.

```
from flask import request


@app.before_request

def log_request_info():

 app.logger.debug('Headers: %s', request.headers)

 app.logger.debug('Body: %s', request.get_data())
```

This function logs headers and body of every incoming request, which can be very helpful for debugging issues related to specific HTTP requests.

Custom Loggers

For larger applications, or those with more complex logging needs, you might want to set up custom loggers for different parts of your application:

```python
custom_logger = logging.getLogger('custom_logger')
file_handler = logging.FileHandler('logs/custom.log')
file_handler.setLevel(logging.INFO)
file_handler.setFormatter(logging.Formatter(
 '%(asctime)s - %(name)s - %(levelname)s - %(message)s'
))
custom_logger.addHandler(file_handler)


@app.route('/')
def index():
 custom_logger.info('Index page is accessed.')
 return "Hello, World!"
```

This setup allows for targeted logging that doesn't pollute the main application log with too much granular data.

Performance Optimization Techniques

For your web app to work smoothly and grow well even when the traffic spikes, you need to optimize its performance in Flask. We will optimize Flask apps by running through several strategies that are useful for database interactions and request handling in particular.

Database Optimization

Query Optimization

- Instead of using **SELECT** *, specify only the columns you need. This reduces the amount of data transferred, parsed, and used in your application.

```
from models import User

users = User.query.with_entities(User.name,
User.email).all()
```

- Ensure that columns used in **WHERE**, **ORDER BY**, and **JOIN** conditions are indexed. This can significantly speed up query execution by reducing the number of records the database needs to scan.

Batch Inserts and Updates

- When inserting or updating multiple rows, batch them into a single operation instead of executing one query per row. This reduces the number of round-trips to the database.

```
from app import db

from models import User


users = [User(name="User1"), User(name="User2"),
User(name="User3")]

db.session.add_all(users)

db.session.commit()
```

- You may also use connection pooling to reuse existing database connections, rather than opening a new connection per request. Flask-SQLAlchemy automatically handles connection pooling.

Request Handling Optimization

Efficient Data Serialization

When your application needs to send or receive large amounts of data, optimize how data is serialized and deserialized. For JSON data, libraries like **ujson** or **orjson** offer faster serialization and deserialization compared to Python's built-in **json** module.

```python
import orjson

def default(obj):
 if isinstance(obj, Decimal):
 return str(obj)
 raise TypeError


json_data = orjson.dumps(data, default=default)
```

Asynchronous Handlers

Consider using asynchronous request handlers for I/O-bound operations. Flask does not support asynchronous views natively, but you can integrate with libraries like **gunicorn** with **gevent** or use Flask alternatives like **Quart** that support asyncio.

```python
# Using gunicorn with gevent
# gunicorn myapp:app -k gevent --worker-connections 1000
```

Caching Responses

Implement caching mechanisms to store the results of expensive operations, so that subsequent requests can be served faster. Flask-Caching can be used to cache views or data.

```python
from flask_caching import Cache


cache = Cache(config={'CACHE_TYPE': 'SimpleCache'})
cache.init_app(app)


@app.route('/expensive_data')
@cache.cached(timeout=50)
def get_expensive_data():
```

```
data = calculate_expensive_data()

return jsonify(data)
```

Application and Web Server Configuration

Use a reverse proxy like Nginx to handle client connections and static files. Nginx can also cache responses, load balance requests among several application instances, and manage slow client connections, all of which help to reduce the load on your Flask application.

```
location /static {

 alias /path/to/your/application/static;

}


location / {

 proxy_pass http://localhost:8000;

 proxy_set_header Host $host;

 proxy_set_header X-Real-IP $remote_addr;

}
```

Monitoring and Profiling

Use tools like New Relic or Prometheus to monitor your application's performance. These tools can help identify bottlenecks and areas that need optimization. Profile your Flask application to pinpoint the most resource-intensive parts. Python's built-in **cProfile** module or tools like **py-spy** can be used for profiling.

```
import cProfile

import pstats


profiler = cProfile.Profile()
```

```
profiler.enable()


# run your code here


profiler.disable()
stats = pstats.Stats(profiler).sort_stats('cumtime')
stats.print_stats()
```

These optimization approaches can help you make your Flask application faster and more scalable by improving its performance. If you follow these steps, you can be confident that your software will be able to manage more users and improve their experience.

Integrating Flask Applications with Docker

You can simplify deployment, guarantee consistency across environments, and streamline development by integrating Docker with your Flask application. In a Docker container, all of a program's executable files, including its code, runtime, system tools, and libraries, are contained therein. This means that Docker containers can hold any program that can be installed on a server. Because of this, you may rest assured that the software will function consistently in any setting.

Installing Docker

Before you can containerize your Flask application, you need to install Docker on your machine. You can install Docker using your package manager. You would run:

```
sudo apt update

sudo apt install docker.io
```

Start and automate the Docker service.

```
sudo systemctl start docker

sudo systemctl enable docker
```

After installing Docker, the next step is to containerize your Flask application. This involves creating a **Dockerfile**, which is a text document that contains all the commands a user could call on the command line to assemble an image.

Create a Dockerfile

Navigate to the root directory of your Flask application and create a file named **Dockerfile**:

```
# Use an official Python runtime as a parent image
FROM python:3.8-slim


# Set the working directory in the container
WORKDIR /app


# Copy the current directory contents into the container at /app
COPY . /app


# Install any needed packages specified in requirements.txt
RUN pip install --no-cache-dir -r requirements.txt


# Make port 80 available to the world outside this container
EXPOSE 80


# Define environment variable
ENV NAME World
```

```
# Run app.py when the container launches
CMD ["python", "app.py"]
```

This **Dockerfile** starts with a Python 3.8 image. The **WORKDIR** sets the working directory within the container. The **COPY** command takes the application source code and copies it into the container. Dependencies are installed using **pip**. The **EXPOSE** command makes the port 80 available outside the container. **CMD** specifies what command to run within the container.

Create .dockerignore file

Just like **.gitignore**, a **.dockerignore** file prevents your local modules and debug logs from being copied onto your Docker image and possibly overwriting modules installed within your image.

```
__pycache__/
*.pyc
*.pyo
*.pyd
.DS_Store
.git
.gitignore
venv/
```

Build Docker Image

From the directory containing the Dockerfile, run the following command to build the Docker image. The **-t** flag lets you tag your image so it's easier to find later using the **docker images** command:

```
docker build -t yourusername/yourappname .
```

Run the Docker Container

After building the image, run it in a Docker container:

```
docker run -p 4000:80 yourusername/yourappname
```

This command maps the port 4000 on your local machine to port 80 on the Docker container, allowing you to access the Flask application via **localhost:4000** in your browser.

Testing the Docker Container

To ensure your Docker container is running correctly, navigate to **http://localhost:4000** in your web browser. You should see your Flask application running as configured.

Through the use of Docker containers, Flask applications can be easily deployed and maintained consistent across development, testing, and production environments. This eliminates the "it works on my machine" issue. The Flask environment and its dependencies are encapsulated by Docker, which makes the application easy to deploy and manage regardless of the underlying native OS or platform.

Summary

This chapter dove further into the more advanced parts of developing and administering Flask applications, expanding on the core knowledge of Flask covered in previous chapters. In order to make the codebase more manageable and scalable, we looked into using Flask Blueprints to structure larger applications. Our capacity to efficiently manage various setups and settings was enhanced as we reviewed the implementation of the Factory paradigm.

Next, we dove into Flask-RESTful, a RESTful service creation framework that simplifies the process of developing RESTful web APIs. Among these tasks was the direct handling of HTTP methods and the organization of answers according to resources. Then we moved on to user authentication and authorization, with the goal of managing access control and establishing ways to confirm user identities. This would guarantee that only authorized users could access resources.

The session also touched on error management and logging, which are important for keeping the program reliable and usable. It included ways for effectively managing and reporting application failures. Subsequently, we looked at performance optimization strategies, which provided ways to make our Flask apps more dynamic and efficient. To achieve these goals, we optimized database interactions and request processing, two components crucial to reducing load times and efficiently managing large numbers of user requests.

At last, we mastered the art of Docker containerization for Flask apps, which streamlines deployment and guarantees consistency in various settings. Our Flask applications were used to create Docker images, which were then launched as containers. Developing professional and scalable web apps with Flask is vital, and this chapter focused on advanced strategies and patterns to help with that. Developers aiming to improve Flask applications and handle bigger projects more efficiently may find these insights essential.

CHAPTER 4: INTRODUCTION TO FASTAPI

Introduction

In this chapter, we'll take a look at FastAPI, a state-of-the-art web framework that uses normal Python type hints to develop APIs with Python 3.6+. It's fast and has good performance. Whether you're coming from Flask or another Python framework, this chapter will help you make the switch to FastAPI and get a feel for its robust capabilities and the benefits it offers to contemporary web development, especially when it comes to creating RESTful APIs.

To kick things off, we'll give you the rundown on switching to FastAPI. In it, you'll find out what sets FastAPI apart from Flask and how those changes can improve your development workflow. Asynchronous programming and type hints are two examples of how contemporary Python capabilities are used by FastAPI. These features improve performance and developer productivity.

The next section teaches how to build RESTful APIs with FastAPI, demonstrating how the library streamlines endpoint definition using Python functions, cuts down on boilerplate code, and makes use of automatic data validation with Pydantic models. Because of this, creating APIs that follow the REST architecture is a breeze.

Next, we'll take a look at FastAPI's Dependency Injection mechanism, which is both simple and powerful, and see how it handles dependencies. You can easily share common functionality across your application, such as database connections and security schemes, with this capability.

In order to handle async database activities, Advanced Database Integration with SQLAlchemy shows how to integrate FastAPI with SQLAlchemy. In this section, we will also look at how to use ORMs to make the most of FastAPI's asynchronous features for efficient database interactions.

If you need to send emails or process data but don't want to impede client responses, you can utilize FastAPI's background task implementation, as shown in Implementing Background Tasks. The last section, "FastAPI and Docker Integration," goes over how to containerize FastAPI apps for easier deployment and more consistent environments in production, testing, and development.

Learn all you need to know about FastAPI's features to create web apps that are secure, scalable, and fast in this detailed chapter. At the end of the book, readers should have all the information they need to begin utilizing FastAPI in their own projects or to think about migrating their current apps to take advantage of FastAPI's sleek design and feature set.

Transitioning to FastAPI

To make the switch from Flask or another web framework to FastAPI, you need to be familiar with its defining features and the benefits it provides. FastAPI is a state-of-the-art web framework that makes use of Python's newest features to facilitate the development of APIs that are both fast and easy to use.

Key Differences Between FastAPI and Flask

Performance

- Asynchronous Support: FastAPI is built on Starlette for the web parts and uses Pydantic for the data parts. It is designed to be asynchronous and can run with Uvicorn, an ASGI server, to support asynchronous request handling out of the box. This makes it inherently faster than Flask, which is a WSGI framework primarily synchronous in nature.

Type Hints and Automatic Data Validation

- FastAPI heavily uses Python type hints for variable declarations. This feature is not just for development clarity but is integral to how FastAPI operates. It uses these type hints to perform data validation and serialization automatically.

```python
from fastapi import FastAPI

from pydantic import BaseModel


app = FastAPI()


class Item(BaseModel):
 name: str

 description: str = None

 price: float

 tax: float = None


@app.post("/items/")

async def create_item(item: Item):
 return {"name": item.name, "price": item.price}
```

In the above sample program, FastAPI uses Pydantic models (**Item** class) to automatically handle data conversion from request data to Python types, validate data, and generate documentation.

Dependency Injection

- FastAPI introduces a dependency injection system that is simple to use yet extremely powerful. This system allows you to have reusable dependencies that can be injected into your route functions.

```python
from fastapi import Depends, FastAPI


def get_db():
  db = DBSession()

  try:

  yield db

  finally:

  db.close()


@app.get("/items/")
async def read_items(db = Depends(get_db)):
  items = db.get_items()

  return items
```

In the above code snippet, **Depends** is used to create a dependency that retrieves a database session for each request, ensuring that the session is closed after the request is complete.

Built-in Interactive API Documentation

- Automatic API Docs: FastAPI automatically generates interactive API documentation using Swagger UI and ReDoc. These docs include live "Try it out" features and are generated from your code with all your API's descriptions, parameter types, and more.

Modern Python Features

- FastAPI is built to work with modern Python versions and features. It inherently supports asynchronous programming which is a perfect match for I/O-bound tasks frequently seen in web API systems.

Understanding these fundamental differences allows you to use its performance benefits and modern Python features to improve your web applications.

Building RESTful APIs with FastAPI

FastAPI's built-in functionalities are designed specifically for the purpose of efficiently creating and managing APIs. By utilizing modern Python features and FastAPI's built-in functionalities, it is possible to fully utilize the capabilities of RESTful APIs. In this section, we'll look at how to make good use of FastAPI to build RESTful APIs, showcasing how it improves and streamlines the process when compared to the old ways.

Defining RESTful Endpoints

FastAPI makes it straightforward to define RESTful endpoints. Here, each endpoint corresponds to an HTTP method and a path. You use decorators to link your Python functions to these paths and methods.

Following is how we define a simple API with GET and POST methods using FastAPI:

```python
from fastapi import FastAPI

from pydantic import BaseModel


app = FastAPI()


class Item(BaseModel):
  name: str

  description: str = None

  price: float

  tax: float = None


@app.get("/")
async def read_root():
```

```
  return {"Hello": "World"}


@app.get("/items/{item_id}")

async def read_item(item_id: int):

 return {"item_id": item_id}


@app.post("/items/")

async def create_item(item: Item):

 return {"name": item.name, "price": item.price}
```

In the above sample program:

- @app.get("/") and @app.get("/items/{item_id}") are endpoints for reading data.
- **@app.post("/items/")** is an endpoint for creating data, using a Pydantic model (**Item**) to automatically handle data validation and serialization.

Path Parameters and Query Strings

FastAPI provides a simple method for defining path parameters and query strings, essential for creating dynamic endpoints.

Path Parameters

- You can define path parameters as function arguments. FastAPI automatically interprets the type annotations to validate and convert input data.

```
@app.get("/users/{user_id}")

async def read_user(user_id: int):

 return {"user_id": user_id}
```

Query Parameters

- Query parameters can be defined as optional function arguments. If a default value is set, the parameter is optional; otherwise, it's required.

```python
@app.get("/items/")

async def read_items(q: str = None):

 query = {"q": q}

 return query
```

Using Request Body

For more complex data, FastAPI allows you to easily handle JSON bodies using Pydantic models, which provide data validation and structure.

```python
@app.put("/items/{item_id}")

async def update_item(item_id: int, item: Item):

 return {"item_id": item_id, "name": item.name, "price": item.price}
```

In the above code snippet, **item** is a Pydantic model instance, parsed from the request body, validated, and serialized directly.

Response Handling

FastAPI provides sophisticated response handling mechanisms, allowing fine control over the HTTP responses.

Custom Status Codes

You can specify the HTTP status code directly in the route decorator or within the return statement.

```python
@app.post("/items/", status_code=201)

async def create_item(item: Item):

 return item
```

Response Headers

Modify response headers by returning a **Response** object.

```python
from fastapi import Response


@app.get("/items/{item_id}")

async def read_item(item_id: int):

 return Response(content=f"Item ID: {item_id}",
media_type="text/plain")
```

Handling Errors

To handle errors in a RESTful API, FastAPI allows you to raise HTTP exceptions that can include custom headers and content.

```python
from fastapi import HTTPException


@app.get("/items/{item_id}")

async def read_item(item_id: int):

 if item_id not in item_db:

 raise HTTPException(status_code=404, detail="Item not found")

 return {"item": item_db[item_id]}
```

This raises an HTTP 404 error if an item is not found, providing a clear error message.

A significant help in the process of rapidly developing and maintaining APIs is provided by the framework's intuitive use of decorators and automatic documentation. Because of this, FastAPI is a significant option for programmers who want to build RESTful services that are both fast and scalable.

Dependency Injection

One design pattern that helps with Inversion of Control (IoC) is Dependency Injection. It makes the system easier to test, manage, and modularize. To ensure that route handlers and other components of the application run smoothly, developers can use dependency injection within the FastAPI framework to define and manage the dependencies that are essential to their work.

Understanding Dependency Injection in FastAPI

FastAPI's dependency injection system works by declaring specific dependencies directly in the path operation function's parameters. These dependencies are then resolved by FastAPI during the request handling process. The framework uses Python type hints to determine what needs to be injected.

How Dependency Injection Works in FastAPI?

Defining Dependencies

Dependencies in FastAPI are typically defined as functions. These functions can perform a variety of tasks, such as fetching database connections, authenticating users, or any other repeatable need across different parts of the application.

```python
from fastapi import Depends, HTTPException


def get_db():
 try:
 db = Database.connect()
 yield db
 finally:
 db.disconnect()


def get_current_user(db=Depends(get_db)):
 user_id = db.get_current_user_id()
 if not user_id:
```

```
raise HTTPException(status_code=404, detail="User not
found")

return user_id
```

In the above code snippet, **get_db** is a dependency that provides a database connection, and **get_current_user** is a dependency that uses another dependency (**get_db**) to fetch the current user's ID from the database.

Using Dependencies in Route Handlers

Once defined, dependencies can be injected into path operations by declaring them as default parameters using the **Depends** class.

```
from fastapi import FastAPI, Depends


app = FastAPI()


@app.get("/users/me")

def read_current_user(user_id: int =
Depends(get_current_user)):

return {"user_id": user_id}
```

In the above sample program, **read_current_user** is a route handler that depends on the **get_current_user** function. FastAPI resolves these dependencies in the background and injects the result (**user_id**) into the path operation function.

Handling Dependencies in Larger Applications

In larger FastAPI applications, you might have multiple dependencies that need to be resolved in different parts of your application. FastAPI allows you to structure these dependencies in a hierarchical manner, where high-level dependencies can rely on lower-level ones.

```
def get_api_key(db=Depends(get_db)):

key = db.get_api_key()
```

```
  if not key:

   raise HTTPException(status_code=403, detail="API key
invalid")

   return key


@app.get("/data")

def read_data(api_key: str = Depends(get_api_key)):

   return {"data": "secret data"}
```

In this setup, **read_data** depends on **get_api_key**, which in turn depends on **get_db**. This hierarchy is automatically resolved by FastAPI, ensuring that each function gets the dependencies it needs to operate effectively. FastAPI's built-in support for dependency injection using simple Python functions and the **Depends** class simplifies what could otherwise be a complex and cumbersome part of application development.

Advanced Database Integration with SQLAlchemy

Object-Relational Mapping (ORM) allows for powerful data manipulation and retrieval operations, and FastAPI applications gain access to SQLAlchemy's advanced database management capabilities through this integration. This integration makes it easy to use Python code to interact with different databases and takes advantage of SQLAlchemy's capabilities for advanced querying, transactions, and more.

Setting up SQLAlchemy with FastAPI

Install Necessary Packages

First, ensure you have SQLAlchemy and databases packages installed which supports async operations:

```
pip install sqlalchemy databases[sqlite]
```

```
pip install asyncpg # For PostgreSQL; for other
databases, install the appropriate driver
```

Configure Database URL

Define your database connection string, which SQLAlchemy will use to connect to your database. This can be configured in your application settings or directly in your code.

```
DATABASE_URL = "sqlite:///./test.db"

# For PostgreSQL:
postgresql://user:password@localhost/dbname
```

Create Database and Tables

Using SQLAlchemy's ORM, define your models which SQLAlchemy uses to create tables in your database. Following is an example model setup:

```
from sqlalchemy import create_engine, Column, Integer,
String, MetaData

from sqlalchemy.ext.declarative import declarative_base

from sqlalchemy.orm import sessionmaker


SQLALCHEMY_DATABASE_URL = "sqlite:///./test.db"

engine = create_engine(SQLALCHEMY_DATABASE_URL,
connect_args={"check_same_thread": False})

SessionLocal = sessionmaker(autocommit=False,
autoflush=False, bind=engine)


Base = declarative_base()


class User(Base):
```

```python
    __tablename__ = "users"

    id = Column(Integer, primary_key=True, index=True)

    username = Column(String, unique=True, index=True)

    email = Column(String, index=True)

    full_name = Column(String)

    disabled = Column(Boolean, default=False)


# Create the database tables

Base.metadata.create_all(bind=engine)
```

This code sets up a SQLite database, defines a **User** model, and creates the corresponding table in the database.

Integrating SQLAlchemy with FastAPI

To integrate SQLAlchemy into your FastAPI application, you typically use dependency injection to provide a session scope around each request.

Database Session Dependency

Create a dependency that you can use in your route handlers to get a session for handling database operations.

```python
from fastapi import Depends, FastAPI, HTTPException

from sqlalchemy.orm import Session


app = FastAPI()


# Dependency

def get_db():
```

```python
db = SessionLocal()

try:

yield db

finally:

db.close()
```

Performing Database Operations

Use the session provided by your dependency to perform CRUD operations. Following is how you might retrieve data from the database:

```python
@app.get("/users/{user_id}", response_model=UserSchema)

async def read_user(user_id: int, db: Session =
Depends(get_db)):

  db_user = db.query(User).filter(User.id ==
user_id).first()

  if db_user is None:

  raise HTTPException(status_code=404, detail="User not
found")

  return db_user
```

Asynchronous Handling

For truly asynchronous handling of database operations in FastAPI, you need to use **databases** package along with SQLAlchemy core (not ORM). This approach allows you to run database queries asynchronously.

Setup Asynchronous Database Connection

```python
from databases import Database
```

```
database = Database(DATABASE_URL)
```

Connect and Disconnect Events

```
@app.on_event("startup")

async def startup():

 await database.connect()


@app.on_event("shutdown")

async def shutdown():

 await database.disconnect()
```

Using Asynchronous Queries

Execute database queries asynchronously using the **database** object.

```
@app.get("/items/")

async def read_items():

 query = items.select()

 return await database.fetch_all(query)
```

More sophisticated, efficient, and scalable applications are made possible with this configuration by utilizing SQLAlchemy ORM's robust routing and object handling features or SQLAlchemy core's asynchronous query execution.

Implementing Background Tasks

Basics of Background Tasks in FastAPI

One efficient method to deal with operations that take a long time or aren't critical for the main response of a request is to implement them in the background of a FastAPI application. Example tasks include sending emails, processing files, or updating databases, where the user should not be delayed before receiving a response.

FastAPI provides a simple and intuitive way to define background tasks that are executed after a response has been sent to the client. This functionality is built directly into FastAPI and uses standard Python features, making it easy to implement without the need for external libraries.

How to Define Background Tasks?

FastAPI includes a **BackgroundTasks** class that can be used to add background tasks to be executed after the request is completed.

Here's how to use it:

```python
from fastapi import FastAPI, BackgroundTasks


app = FastAPI()


def write_log(message: str):
  with open("log.txt", "a") as log:
  log.write(f"{message}\n")


@app.post("/send-notification/")
async def send_notification(email: str, background_tasks:
BackgroundTasks):
  background_tasks.add_task(write_log,
message=f"notification sent to {email}")
  return {"message": "Notification sent in the
background"}
```

In the above sample program, when the **/send-notification/** endpoint is called, it schedules the **write_log** function to run in the background. The API immediately responds with a message to the user, while the logging operation is performed without making the user wait.

Implementing More Complex Background Operations

For more complex or resource-heavy background tasks, you might need to integrate a more robust solution like Celery with a message broker such as RabbitMQ or Redis. Given below is a basic outline of how this could be implemented:

Setting up Celery

Install Celery and choose a message broker (RabbitMQ, Redis, etc.), then set up Celery in your FastAPI application.

```python
from celery import Celery


def make_celery(app):
 celery = Celery(
 app.import_name,
 backend=app.config['CELERY_RESULT_BACKEND'],
 broker=app.config['CELERY_BROKER_URL']
 )
 celery.conf.update(app.config)


 class ContextTask(celery.Task):
 def __call__(self, *args, **kwargs):
 with app.app_context():
 return self.run(*args, **kwargs)


 celery.Task = ContextTask
 return celery
```

```
celery = make_celery(app)
```

Define Celery Tasks

You can define tasks that Celery will handle asynchronously. Given below is how to define a simple Celery task.

```
@celery.task()

def send_email(email: str):

 # logic to send an email

 pass
```

Trigger Celery Tasks from FastAPI

You can now trigger these Celery tasks from your FastAPI routes as needed.

```
@app.post("/send-email/")

async def send_email_endpoint(email: str):

 send_email.delay(email=email)

 return {"message": "Email is being sent in the
background"}
```

The built-in BackgroundTasks in FastAPI are easily usable and more than enough for basic tasks. In more intricate situations, a task queue such as Celery is better suited for tasks that necessitate strong management, scalability, or distributed processing.

FastAPI and Docker Integration

One way to use Docker with FastAPI is to containerize your FastAPI app. This will make it easier to test, develop, and launch your app in distinct but compatible environments. The FastAPI app and all of its dependencies are encapsulated into a Docker container during this process. The container can then be easily deployed and managed.

Installing Docker

Before containerizing the FastAPI application, ensure Docker is installed in your development environment as below.

```
sudo apt update

sudo apt install docker.io

sudo systemctl start docker

sudo systemctl enable docker
```

After installation, add your user to the Docker group to run Docker commands without **sudo**.

```
sudo usermod -aG docker ${USER}

su - ${USER}
```

Creating a Dockerfile for FastAPI

To containerize your FastAPI application, create a Dockerfile in the root directory of your FastAPI project. This file defines the steps to build the Docker image as below.

```
# Use an official Python runtime as the base image

FROM python:3.8


# Set the working directory in the container

WORKDIR /code


# Copy the current directory contents into the container at /code

COPY ./ /code
```

```
# Install any needed packages specified in
requirements.txt

RUN pip install --no-cache-dir -r requirements.txt


# Make port 8000 available to the world outside this
container

EXPOSE 8000


# Define environment variable

ENV NAME World


# Run the application

CMD ["uvicorn", "main:app", "--host", "0.0.0.0", "--
port", "8000"]
```

The above script demonstrates:

- The Dockerfile starts with a Python 3.8 image.
- Sets up a working directory **/code** inside the container.
- Copies the FastAPI application into the Docker container.
- Installs dependencies from **requirements.txt**.
- Exposes port 8000 for the Uvicorn server.
- Runs the FastAPI application using Uvicorn.

Building the Docker Image

Navigate to the directory containing your Dockerfile and run the following command to build the Docker image:

```
docker build -t fastapi-app .
```

This command builds the Docker image using the Dockerfile in the current directory, tagging the image as **fastapi-app**.

Running FastAPI App in Docker Container

Once the image is built, run your FastAPI application in a Docker container using:

```
docker run -d -p 8000:8000 fastapi-app
```

The **-d** flag runs the container in detached mode, letting it run in the background. And, the **-p 8000:8000** maps port 8000 of the container to port 8000 on the host, allowing you to access the FastAPI application via **localhost:8000**.

Verify Application

To ensure your FastAPI application is running correctly in Docker, navigate to **http://localhost:8000** in your web browser. You should see your FastAPI application responding as configured.

After following these steps, you should be able to run your FastAPI app in a Docker container. You have also successfully set up a Docker environment. With this configuration, your application will always run in a sandbox, independent of any other environment, whether it's a local machine, a test environment, or a production server.

Summary

An up-to-date web framework for creating high-performance APIs with Python, FastAPI was thoroughly introduced in this chapter. First, we looked at how FastAPI replaced Flask, focusing on FastAPI's asynchronous programming support and its type hint and Pydantic library–based automatic data validation capabilities. With this groundwork in place, we could go more deeply into the details of RESTful API development with FastAPI. After that, we dove into how FastAPI makes RESTful service development easier. By eliminating the need for repetitive code, it streamlines common processes like request processing, data validation, and response serialization. This simplified method boosts application performance and dependability while simultaneously increasing developer productivity.

Another significant topic that we covered was dependency injection. By handling dependencies through reusable functions, FastAPI's advanced dependency injection system makes code cleaner and easier to maintain. Database connections and user authentication are examples of common patterns, and this system is crucial for efficiently handling them. This chapter also goes over SQLAlchemy's advanced database integration with FastAPI settings, with a focus on asynchronous database operations to make the most of FastAPI's non-blocking features. Fast and scalable database interactions are guaranteed by this integration.

In addition, we gained knowledge about how to use FastAPI's background tasks, which are crucial for processes that run too long to be contained in the request-response cycle. Tasks like sending emails or processing big data files can run in parallel without slowing down the main application flow, ensuring that the user experience remains fluid. A demonstration on how to integrate FastAPI applications with Docker was the last section of the chapter. Here we covered how to containerize a FastAPI app, which means wrapping it in Docker for easier deployment and cross-environment scalability. Whether the application is in production, testing, or development, this guarantees consistency.

In sum, this chapter taught readers how to use FastAPI to create web applications that are strong, efficient, and simple to deploy.

CHAPTER 5: WORKING WITH DATABASES

Introduction

Building reliable and extensible web apps requires a thorough understanding of database management and optimization strategies, both of which are covered extensively in this chapter. This chapter delves into advanced techniques for interacting with databases, covering a wide range of technologies and methodologies from classic relational databases to contemporary NoSQL systems.

First, we'll take a look at MySQL and PostgreSQL, two of the relational databases that are widely used. All the details regarding the characteristics, advantages, and recommended applications of each database management system are laid out here. Learn more about the pros and cons of each option and how to pick the right one for your application from this chapter. Then, we'll take a look at NoSQL databases, specifically MongoDB, which is well-known for its scalability, high availability, and excellent performance. You will learn the ropes of working with MongoDB, from its document-oriented structure to its substantial differences from relational databases in data modeling and retrieval to its advantages and disadvantages.

The fundamentals of database design are subsequently covered in the chapter. Data integrity, improved performance, and easier database system maintenance are all outcomes of well-designed databases. Database schema design that is both efficient and dependable requires knowledge of normalization, relationships, and key constraints. We will then explore more complex querying methods and CRUD (Create, Read, Update, Delete) operations. In this part, you will learn to work with more complicated data structures, retrieve data in more complex ways, write better queries, and manipulate data more effectively across various database systems.

After that, we'll learn about version control and database migrations. In order to keep development, testing, and production environments consistent, you will learn how to manage and track changes in the database schema over time. Object-Relational Mapping (ORM) systems in Python and database integration is another important topic. This section explains how ORMs simplify database interactions by making it possible to work with database entities as Python objects. This helps to simplify developer productivity by removing complex SQL queries.

The chapter wraps up by going over some caching strategies that can help optimize databases. By lowering the database's workload and data retrieval latency, caching works wonders for database-driven applications' performance. In this chapter, you will learn all you need to know to create high-performing web apps, including how to manage databases, manipulate data effectively, and optimize database interactions.

MySQL and PostgreSQL

Data storage, retrieval, and manipulation capabilities offered by relational databases make them the foundation of many contemporary web applications. Among relational databases, PostgreSQL and MySQL are among the most widely used. Despite their similarities and extensive SQL support, there are a number of ways in which these two databases differ that could make one better suited to your needs than the other.

MySQL

MySQL is an open-source relational database management system known for its reliability and ease of use. It is particularly popular in web applications and is part of the LAMP (Linux, Apache, MySQL, PHP/Python/Perl) stack. MySQL is generally considered fast and efficient for read-heavy applications. It uses a default storage engine called InnoDB, which offers full ACID (Atomicity, Consistency, Isolation, Durability) compliance and supports transactions, which are critical for maintaining data integrity.

MySQL supports master-slave replication, allowing data from one MySQL database server (the master) to be replicated to one or more MySQL database servers (the slaves). Replication is primarily used for scale-out strategies, data backup, and redundancy. MySQL is known for its simplicity and ease of use. It can be a good choice for small to medium web projects that need a database that's easy to set up and manage.

PostgreSQL

PostgreSQL, often simply Postgres, is an open-source relational database management system that emphasizes extensibility and SQL compliance. It is considered to be more advanced than MySQL in terms of technology and features. PostgreSQL is highly regarded for its ability to handle complex queries and extensive concurrency. It supports a variety of performance enhancers such as indexes with expressions, partial indexes, and an extensive set of index types. PostgreSQL supports advanced data types and sophisticated performance optimization that can handle complex, high-volume environments. This includes geospatial data through PostGIS, custom data types, and sophisticated locking mechanisms.

PostgreSQL is highly extensible. For example, you can define your own data types, build out custom functions, even write code from different programming languages without recompiling your database. PostgreSQL is known for its high level of ACID compliance. It supports complex SQL transactions and focuses heavily on conformity with the SQL standard.

Choosing Between MySQL and PostgreSQL

When deciding whether to use MySQL or PostgreSQL for your Python backend application, consider the following aspects:

Application Requirements

- If your application requires full ACID compliance and sophisticated transactional support, PostgreSQL might be the better choice.

- If your application is read-heavy and not as complex in terms of transactional operations or does not require the advanced features provided by PostgreSQL, MySQL might suffice.

Scalability

- Both databases offer good scalability options, but the choice might depend on the type of scalability needed. For read-heavy applications, MySQL's replication capabilities make it a robust choice.

- PostgreSQL offers better write scalability and is more suitable for applications with a heavy load of concurrent transactions.

Support and Compatibility

- Both MySQL and PostgreSQL have strong communities and extensive documentation. PostgreSQL's community is particularly strong in the open source arena, with a lot of third-party tools and extensions available.

- MySQL, owned by Oracle Corporation, has commercial support available, which can be a deciding factor for enterprises requiring guaranteed support.

- Consider what databases your application needs to interact with. If you're already using tools that integrate better with MySQL or PostgreSQL, this might influence your choice.

Both PostgreSQL and MySQL are great options for Python backends, but they cater to slightly different requirements. Applications necessitating complicated queries, substantial data integrity, or specialized features like support for geographic data may find PostgreSQL more suitable due to its more sophisticated features that are available out of the box. Applications requiring easier replication configurations, faster setup, and good performance under heavy read loads may want to consider MySQL. Decisions should be based on development team technical proficiency, future scalability requirements, and project specific requirements.

MongoDB

Many modern applications that need scalable databases and flexible data structures choose MongoDB, a powerful NoSQL database, because of its high availability, easy scalability, and high performance. In contrast to relational databases, which rely on tables and a predetermined schema, MongoDB is document-oriented. This allows for a more versatile and adaptable data model, as data is stored in BSON documents (Binary JSON) with a dynamic schema.

Understanding MongoDB and Its Document Model

MongoDB uses a document model, which is a semi-structured data format. This model is incredibly flexible, allowing you to store data without needing to define the structure beforehand. Each document can have its own unique structure with different fields, and the data type of each field can vary from document to document.

Documents

These are the basic units of data in MongoDB, akin to rows in a relational database, but much more flexible. A document in MongoDB is a map of field names to values. These values can include arrays and nested documents, providing the ability to store complex hierarchical structures with a single document.

Collections

Collections are analogous to tables in relational databases. They can hold multiple documents. Unlike tables in relational databases, a collection does not enforce schema constraints, which means different documents in a collection can have different fields.

Why Choose MongoDB?

- Scalability: MongoDB is designed with scalability in mind. It supports horizontal scaling through sharding, distributing data across multiple machines.

- Performance: MongoDB offers high performance for both reads and writes. Its storage engine is optimized for powerful storage and retrieval of data, which enhances overall performance.

- Flexibility: Thanks to its schema-less design, MongoDB allows you to develop applications without having to pre-define the schema or modify it extensively as new requirements arise.

- High Availability: MongoDB's replication facility, called replica sets, provides automatic failover and data redundancy, which guarantees that your application is highly available.

MongoDB's Key Features

1. MongoDB supports searching by field, range queries, and regular expression searches. Queries can return specific fields within documents and include user-defined JavaScript functions.

2. Any field in a MongoDB document can be indexed. Indices are critical for improving the performance of searches.

3. MongoDB provides an aggregation framework based on the concept of data processing pipelines. Documents enter a multi-stage pipeline that transforms the documents into aggregated results.

4. For storing and retrieving large files such as images, videos, or large blobs of data, MongoDB provides GridFS, a specification for storing and retrieving files that exceed the BSON-document size limit of 16MB.

Integrating MongoDB

To use MongoDB with Python, you will typically use the **pymongo** library, which provides tools for working with MongoDB.

Installation

Install **pymongo** using pip.

```
pip install pymongo
```

Connecting to MongoDB

Create a Python script that connects to your MongoDB instance.

```
from pymongo import MongoClient


# Connect to the MongoDB server running on localhost at port 27017

client = MongoClient('localhost', 27017)


# Access the database named 'test_database'

db = client.test_database
```

Operations

- Creating and Inserting Documents.

```
# Access the collection named 'test_collection'

collection = db.test_collection


# Insert a document

post = {"author": "John", "text": "First post!"}
```

```
collection.insert_one(post)
```

- Querying.

```
# Find a single document
import pprint

pprint.pprint(collection.find_one({"author": "John"}))
```

- Updating.

```
# Update a document
collection.update_one({"author": "John"}, {"$set":
{"text": "Updated post"}})
```

- Deleting.

```
# Delete a document
collection.delete_one({"author": "John"})
```

Its adaptability to various data types, deep query-ability, and inherent scalability make it an attractive choice for modern applications that demand a strong and versatile database.

Database Design Principles

The development of effective, scalable, and easily maintained databases relies heavily on database design principles. If your database is well-designed, your application will run smoothly and be able to withstand changes as they occur. Data type, anticipated load, and query types are all important considerations when deciding on the optimal database schema for a backend application.

Core Principles of Database Design

Normalization

Normalization is the process of structuring a relational database in accordance with a series of so-called normal forms in order to reduce data redundancy and improve data integrity. Normalization involves decomposing a table into less redundant tables without losing information.

- First Normal Form (1NF): Ensures each column of a table is atomic and each row contains unique data.

- Second Normal Form (2NF): Requires the database to be in 1NF and all columns that are not dependent on the primary key must be removed.

- Third Normal Form (3NF): A database is in 3NF if it is in 2NF and all the columns in a table are not only dependent on the primary key but also independent of each other.

Entity-Relationship Model

An Entity-Relationship (ER) model helps visualize and design the database structure. It involves defining entities (things about which you want to store data) and their relationships to each other.

Practical Database Schema Design

For a backend application, suppose you are developing a system for a university management system where you need to manage students, courses, and the enrollment of students in these courses. Given below is how you could design the database schema:

Entities

- Students: Contains details about the students.

- Courses: Contains information about courses.

- Enrollments: Represents the relationship between students and courses.

Attributes

1. Students:

    - **Student_ID** (Primary Key)
        - **Name**
        - **Email**
        - **Date_of_birth**

2. Courses:

    - **Course_ID** (Primary Key)
        - **Course_Name**
        - **Course_Description**

3. Enrollments:

    - **Enrollment_ID** (Primary Key)

- **Student_ID** (Foreign Key)
- **Course_ID** (Foreign Key)
  - **Enrollment_Date**

This relationship is many-to-many and is represented through the Enrollments table, which includes foreign keys referencing both the Students and Courses tables, establishing a link between the two.

SQL Code for Creating Tables

```
CREATE TABLE Students (

 Student_ID INT PRIMARY KEY,

 Name VARCHAR(100),

 Email VARCHAR(100),

 Date_of_birth DATE

);


CREATE TABLE Courses (

 Course_ID INT PRIMARY KEY,

 Course_Name VARCHAR(100),

 Course_Description TEXT

);


CREATE TABLE Enrollments (

 Enrollment_ID INT PRIMARY KEY,

 Student_ID INT,

 Course_ID INT,
```

```
Enrollment_Date DATE,

  FOREIGN KEY (Student_ID) REFERENCES
Students(Student_ID),

  FOREIGN KEY (Course_ID) REFERENCES Courses(Course_ID)

);
```

Our example university management system's schema is built to efficiently manage student, course, and enrollment data. The backend operations can be executed efficiently and reliably thanks to this design's reduction of redundancy and improvement of database integrity.

CRUD Operations

We shall now dive into the implementation of CRUD operations. The efficient management of data by your application is made possible by these operations. We will explore SQL methods for carrying out these operations on the data contained in our schema that we have created.

Creating Records (CREATE)

To add new data into our tables, we use the SQL **INSERT** statement. Given below is how you can add records to the **Students**, **Courses**, and **Enrollments** tables.

```
-- Inserting data into the Students table

INSERT INTO Students (Student_ID, Name, Email,
Date_of_birth)

VALUES (1, 'John Doe', 'john.doe@gitforgits.com', '2000-
01-01');



-- Inserting data into the Courses table

INSERT INTO Courses (Course_ID, Course_Name,
Course_Description)

VALUES (101, 'Introduction to Psychology', 'A
foundational course covering basic principles of
psychology.');
```

```
-- Inserting data into the Enrollments table

INSERT INTO Enrollments (Enrollment_ID, Student_ID,
Course_ID, Enrollment_Date)

VALUES (1, 1, 101, '2021-09-01');
```

These SQL statements add a student, a course, and a record of enrollment linking the student to the course.

Reading Records (READ)

Reading data, or querying tables, is done using the SQL **SELECT** statement. Below are examples of how to retrieve data from the tables.

```
-- Select all fields from Students

SELECT * FROM Students;
```

```
-- Select a specific course by ID

SELECT * FROM Courses WHERE Course_ID = 101;
```

```
-- Select all enrollments including student and course
details

SELECT s.Name, c.Course_Name, e.Enrollment_Date

FROM Enrollments e

JOIN Students s ON e.Student_ID = s.Student_ID

JOIN Courses c ON e.Course_ID = c.Course_ID;
```

These queries demonstrate how to retrieve all students, specific courses, and detailed enrollment records including the names of the students and the courses they are enrolled in.

Updating Records (UPDATE)

Modifying existing records is achieved using the **UPDATE** statement. Given below is how to update data in the **Students** and **Courses** tables.

```
-- Update email for a student

UPDATE Students

SET Email = 'new.email@gitforgits.com'

WHERE Student_ID = 1;
```

```
-- Update course description

UPDATE Courses

SET Course_Description = 'An updated description of the
course.'

WHERE Course_ID = 101;
```

These statements change a student's email and update the description of a course.

Deleting Records (DELETE)

Removing records is handled by the **DELETE** statement. Given below is how you can delete from the **Enrollments** table, and the associated cascading considerations.

```
-- Delete an enrollment

DELETE FROM Enrollments

WHERE Enrollment_ID = 1;
```

```
-- Delete a student and all their enrollments

DELETE FROM Students

WHERE Student_ID = 1;
```

```
-- Assuming CASCADE DELETE is set up, otherwise, you need
to manually delete from Enrollments first.
```

When deleting a student, ensure that either the foreign key constraint on enrollments is set to cascade deletes or manually remove the related enrollments to maintain referential integrity.

Considerations for CRUD Operations

For operations that involve multiple steps (like deleting a student and their enrollments), use transactions to ensure that all operations succeed or fail together. This maintains data integrity.

```
BEGIN TRANSACTION;

DELETE FROM Enrollments WHERE Student_ID = 1;

DELETE FROM Students WHERE Student_ID = 1;

COMMIT;
```

To keep the database up-to-date and the application responsive to user inputs, each of the above operations are necessary.

Advanced Querying Techniques

Moving forward from the basic CRUD operations we covered prior to this, let's explore advanced querying techniques that enable more intricate and efficient data retrieval and manipulation. Subqueries, joins, and SQL functions are all part of these techniques, which allow for more complex data analysis and extraction. The primary goal is to enhance the database functionality of the university management system by adding advanced query capabilities beyond basic CRUD operations.

Subqueries

Subqueries are queries nested within another SQL query, often used in the **SELECT**, **FROM**, or **WHERE** clause. They can be used to perform operations that require multiple steps in data filtering or to derive calculations.

Sample Program: Finding Courses with No Enrollments

Suppose you want to find courses that have not been enrolled in by any student. This can be achieved using a subquery to exclude courses that appear in the enrollments table.

```
SELECT Course_ID, Course_Name

FROM Courses

WHERE Course_ID NOT IN (SELECT Course_ID FROM
Enrollments);
```

This query selects courses that do not have a matching entry in the enrollments table, effectively listing courses without students.

Joins

Joins are used to combine rows from two or more tables based on a related column between them. They are essential for queries that need to aggregate data from multiple related entities.

Sample Program: List of Students with Their Courses

To get a detailed list of students along with the courses they are enrolled in, you would use a **JOIN** operation:

```
SELECT s.Name, s.Email, c.Course_Name

FROM Students s

JOIN Enrollments e ON s.Student_ID = e.Student_ID

JOIN Courses c ON e.Course_ID = c.Course_ID;
```

This query provides a comprehensive view of which students are enrolled in which courses, leveraging joins to amalgamate data from three tables.

SQL Aggregate Functions

SQL aggregate functions perform a calculation on a set of values and return a single value. They are used with the **GROUP BY** statement to group rows that have the same values in specified columns into summary rows.

Sample Program: Count of Students Enrolled in Each Course

To determine how popular each course is, you could count the number of students enrolled in each course.

```
SELECT c.Course_Name, COUNT(*) as Student_Count
```

```
FROM Courses c

JOIN Enrollments e ON c.Course_ID = e.Course_ID

GROUP BY c.Course_Name;
```

This query groups the results by course name and counts the number of entries in the enrollments table for each course, giving a count of students per course.

Advanced Filtering with HAVING

The **HAVING** clause is used to filter the results of a **GROUP BY** in aggregate functions. Unlike the **WHERE** clause, **HAVING** can filter aggregated data.

Sample Program: Courses with More Than 5 Students

If you want to find only those courses that have more than 5 students enrolled:

```
SELECT c.Course_Name, COUNT(*) as Student_Count

FROM Courses c

JOIN Enrollments e ON c.Course_ID = e.Course_ID

GROUP BY c.Course_Name

HAVING COUNT(*) > 5;
```

This query lists courses that are particularly popular, having more than 5 students enrolled.

Window Functions

Window functions provide a way to perform calculations across a set of table rows that are somehow related to the current row. This is similar to aggregate functions, but window functions do not cause rows to become grouped into a single output row.

Sample Program: Rank Students by Enrollment Date in Each Course

Suppose you want to rank students based on when they enrolled in each course:

```
SELECT s.Name, c.Course_Name, e.Enrollment_Date,

 RANK() OVER (PARTITION BY e.Course_ID ORDER BY
e.Enrollment_Date) as Enrollment_Rank
```

```
FROM Enrollments e

JOIN Students s ON e.Student_ID = s.Student_ID

JOIN Courses c ON e.Course_ID = c.Course_ID;
```

This query uses a window function to rank students within each course based on their enrollment date, without collapsing the results into a single row per course.

These methods enable more complex queries, which are crucial for comprehensive data analysis and reporting in complicated applications such as the university management system. A more data-driven and dynamic approach to database queries is made possible by these, leading to richer insights and more effective data operations.

Database Migrations and Version Control

Over time, changes to a database schema need to be handled without losing data. This is where database migrations come in. Applications developed in agile development environments frequently necessitate iterative changes to the database structure, making this process essential. For database migrations to be managed well, it is necessary to keep track of all schema changes in a way that can be applied, rolled back, and version controlled with the application code.

Understanding Database Migrations

Database migrations typically include modifications such as adding or dropping tables, altering tables to add or remove columns, or changing indices and constraints. These changes are saved in migration scripts, which are files that can be executed to modify the database schema. These scripts not only update the schema but also ensure that existing data conforms to the new schema without loss.

Various tools exist to facilitate database migrations, each compatible with different types of databases and frameworks. For Python-based applications, particularly those using SQLAlchemy, tools like Alembic are often used. Alembic provides a migration framework for SQLAlchemy which allows you to migrate the database reliably and efficiently.

Setting up Alembic

To set up Alembic for database migration management:

Install Alembic

```
pip install alembic
```

Initialize Alembic

Navigate to your project directory and run:

```
alembic init alembic
```

This command creates a new directory called **alembic** containing your migration scripts and an **alembic.ini** configuration file.

Configure Alembic

Modify the **alembic.ini** file to specify the connection string to your database. You also need to configure the **env.py** file inside the **alembic** directory to define how Alembic connects to your database using SQLAlchemy.

```
from myapp.models import Base # assuming your models are
in myapp/models.py

target_metadata = Base.metadata
```

Creating and Applying Migrations

Once Alembic is set up, you can create and apply migrations:

Create Migration

To generate a new migration script automatically based on the differences between your models and the current database schema, run:

```
alembic revision --autogenerate -m "Description of the
change"
```

This command will add a new script to the **versions** folder within your Alembic directory. Review this script to ensure it accurately represents the desired changes.

Edit Migration Script

Sometimes, automatic generation might not perfectly capture complex changes or specific database operations. In these cases, manually edit the migration script in the **versions** directory to correct or refine the operations.

Apply Migrations

To update the database to the latest version, use:

```
alembic upgrade head
```

This command applies all pending migrations to the database. For rollback, you can use:

```
alembic downgrade -1
```

This command reverts the last applied migration.

Managing Schema Changes

Managing database schema changes with version control involves:

Versioning

Each migration script is timestamped and stored in a version-controlled repository along with your application code. This synchronization allows you to match every state of your application code with the corresponding state of the database schema.

Collaboration

When working in a team, migrations ensure that all members are working with the same database schema. After pulling changes that include new migrations, team members can apply these migrations to their local development databases.

Deployment

During deployment, migrations are applied as part of the deployment process. This ensures that the production database schema matches the schema expected by the deployed version of the application.

Alembic and similar tools make it easy to manage changes across environments and keep application code and database schema consistent, which is crucial for safe and smooth migrations.

Integrating Databases with Python ORMs

Overview of Python ORMs

Python ORMs act as a bridge between Python code and the database, allowing for interaction with the database using Pythonic operations. This eliminates the need for manual SQL query construction for most operations, thus reducing the likelihood of SQL injection attacks and syntax errors. Popular Python ORMs include SQLAlchemy, Django ORM, and Peewee. We will look into SQLAlchemy in this book as I find it a highly featured ORM amongst all the options available.

SQLAlchemy Overview

SQLAlchemy is one of the most feature-rich and flexible ORMs available in the Python ecosystem. It provides full support for relational databases and offers a choice between two distinct usage paradigms: the SQLAlchemy Core and the SQLAlchemy ORM.

SQLAlchemy Core

- The Core is centered around the use of SQL expressions as Python objects, and it is schema-centric. It allows precise control over SQL and is well-suited for complex database operations which don't neatly fit into the Active Record pattern.

SQLAlchemy ORM

- The ORM is the higher-level interface that allows you to deal with models and classes linked to database tables. It includes a system of relationships that can be used to automatically persist changes in objects and their related objects.

Integrating SQLAlchemy ORM with Python

To integrate SQLAlchemy ORM into a Python application, you follow several steps to set up and utilize the ORM to manipulate database entries.

Installation

Begin by installing SQLAlchemy using pip.

```
pip install SQLAlchemy
```

Defining Models

Models in SQLAlchemy are classes that define the structure of a database table. Each attribute of the class corresponds to a column in the database table.

```
from sqlalchemy import create_engine, Column, Integer, String

from sqlalchemy.ext.declarative import declarative_base

from sqlalchemy.orm import sessionmaker
```

```python
Base = declarative_base()


class User(Base):
  __tablename__ = 'users'


  id = Column(Integer, primary_key=True)
  name = Column(String)
  email = Column(String)


# Create an engine that stores data in the local
directory's
engine = create_engine('sqlite:///mydatabase.db')
Base.metadata.create_all(engine)
```

Creating Session

SQLAlchemy uses sessions to manage operations on objects bound to a database. A session establishes all conversations with the database and represents a 'holding zone' for all the objects which you've loaded or associated with it during its lifespan.

```python
Session = sessionmaker(bind=engine)
session = Session()
```

Performing Database Operations

- Create.

```python
new_user = User(name='John Doe',
email='john@gitforgits.com')

session.add(new_user)
```

```
session.commit()
```

- Read.

```
user = session.query(User).filter_by(name='John
Doe').first()
```

```
print(user.email)
```

- Update.

```
user.email = 'new.email@gitforgits.com'
```

```
session.commit()
```

- Delete.

```
session.delete(user)
```

```
session.commit()
```

You can make database interactions much easier in your Python applications by integrating SQLAlchemy. With its ability to abstract away raw SQL queries, it makes code cleaner and more maintainable. Additionally, it offers powerful tools such as automatic schema migrations, relationship management, and unit-of-work implementations, which can handle even the most complex data models.

Caching Strategies for Database Optimization

An essential tactic for improving the speed of apps that rely on databases is caching. This technique involves reducing the need to repeatedly query the database for the same data by temporarily storing copies of the data in fast-access hardware like RAM. This can significantly reduce database load and response times during peak usage times. Here, we'll take a look at various caching strategies that web applications can use to improve their interactions with databases.

Types of Caching

Result Caching

This involves storing the results of database queries. When a query is executed for the first time, its result set is stored in a cache. Subsequent identical queries can be served directly from the cache, skipping the database query phase entirely.

Object Caching

In object caching, data objects are cached instead of raw query results. This is particularly useful in applications using an ORM where data interaction is done through object representations. Object caching can help in rapidly retrieving entity objects without needing to reconstruct them from database query results.

Query Plan Caching

SQL databases often cache query execution plans, which are the strategies the database engine uses to execute queries. Query plan caching avoids the overhead of query optimization during subsequent executions of the same query, thus speeding up the query execution process.

Implementing Caching in Web Applications

Redis as a Cache

Redis is a popular choice for implementing caching in web applications due to its high performance and rich set of data structures. Redis operates entirely in-memory, and it can be used as a result and object cache.

Following is a basic setup for using Redis with a Python web application:

- Install Redis and start the Redis service on your machine or use a Redis cloud service.

- Use the **redis-py** library to integrate Redis caching into your application.

```
pip install redis

import redis

r = redis.Redis(host='localhost', port=6379, db=0) #
Connect to local Redis instance


# Example of setting and retrieving a cache value

r.set('foo', 'bar')

value = r.get('foo')

print(value) # Outputs: b'bar'
```

Caching Strategy

- When a query is executed, store its result in Redis. Use the query string itself as the key for the Redis store.

```
def get_user(user_id):
 # Check if the result is in cache
 result = r.get(f'user_{user_id}')
 if result is None:
 # If not, fetch from database and cache it
 user = query_database(f"SELECT * FROM users WHERE id = {user_id}")
 r.set(f'user_{user_id}', serialize(user))
 return user
 return deserialize(result)
```

- Proper cache invalidation is crucial to prevent stale data from being served. Invalidate or update the cache entry when data modifications occur.

```
def update_user(user_id, new_data):
 # Update database
 update_database(f"UPDATE users SET data = {new_data} WHERE id = {user_id}")
 # Invalidate cache
 r.delete(f'user_{user_id}')
```

Considerations for Effective Caching

- Decide the granularity of caching. Finer granularity (e.g., caching individual objects) can lead to better cache utilization but might increase complexity in cache invalidation.

- Set appropriate cache lifetimes to balance between freshness and performance. Use time-to-live (TTL) settings for cache entries to ensure data does not become too stale.

- Ensure there is consistency between the cache and the database. This can be one of the biggest challenges in cache management, requiring solid strategies for cache invalidation and updates.

- Your application's performance and the database's workload can both be significantly improved with the help of caching strategies. Cache management solutions, such as Redis, allow applications to scale more easily and respond faster by storing frequently requested data in a highly accessible memory location.

Summary

This chapter concentrated on comprehensive database management techniques and optimization strategies that are critical for effective backend development. We started by looking at relational databases, specifically MySQL and PostgreSQL, and going over their basic features and scenarios that help you choose the right one for your project. Next, we moved on to NoSQL databases, specifically highlighting MongoDB due to its adaptability and speed in managing the kinds of massive data operations seen in contemporary applications.

It then moved on to cover the basics of database design, stressing the significance of well-structured databases for data integrity and query performance. To aid in the conceptualization and implementation of strong database schemas, concepts such as normalization and the use of Entity-Relationship models were emphasized.

Additionally, more complex CRUD operations were studied, illustrating improved database interaction. As a means of improving our skills in dynamic data management within the case study university management system, we dove into data creation, reading, updating, and deletion.

This was followed by an practical overview of advanced querying techniques, which included new ways to retrieve data that was more complicated. Several methods were covered to facilitate complex data manipulation and analysis, including subqueries, joins, aggregate functions, and window functions.

To wrap up the chapter, we went over database migrations and version control in detail, highlighting how important they are for managing schema changes in databases over time without losing data. The efficiency of tools such as Alembic in monitoring, implementing, and rolling back database modifications during application development cycles was emphasized.

Lastly, we covered caching strategies that can help optimize databases. We took a look at various caching strategies, such as object caching and result caching, and showed how to apply them with tools like Redis to lessen database load and drastically improve application performance.

In sum, the chapter laid a solid foundation for efficient database management, which is essential for making sure applications work as intended while also being fast and easy to scale.

CHAPTER 6: ASYNCHRONOUS PROGRAMMING IN PYTHON

Introduction

In this chapter, we will explore the inner workings and practical uses of asynchronous programming in the Python environment. In order to help readers become proficient in writing efficient and scalable applications, this chapter will go over Python's asynchronous programming features.

The first stop on the way is a "Asynchronous Programming Overview," in which we go over the basics of asynchronous programming, its benefits, and the situations in which it outshines more conventional synchronous approaches. This lays the groundwork for comprehending the wider effects and uses of this programming approach.

The next section, "Asyncio Basics," will teach you how to use the async/await syntax to write concurrent code in Python. Event loops, tasks, and coroutines—essential for executing asynchronous operations—are covered in this section, along with the other core components of asyncio.

Topics covered in "Developing Asynchronous Web Applications" include the use of asyncio in various web development settings. In this example, we'll show you how to improve the speed and responsiveness of your web apps by managing your structured network code and I/O requests.

Doing database operations at different times is what the section on "Asynchronous Database Access" is all about. In order to keep web applications responsive, it is necessary to implement asyncio with database operations. This will enable non-blocking database queries and updates, which will be covered in this section.

For those unfamiliar with WebSockets and their use in asynchronous contexts, "Implementing Websockets" is a great place to start. An always-on, low-latency connection between client and server is ideal for real-time web apps because it significantly improves the user experience.

When it comes to creating efficient, well-structured, and easily-maintained asynchronous code, "Async Best Practices and Patterns" is a significant resource. This section is designed to assist developers in making the most of Python's async capabilities while avoiding typical mistakes.

Last but not least, "Debugging Asynchronous Applications" teaches methods for solving problems with asynchronous apps, which are notoriously difficult to debug because of the subtleties of concurrent execution.

Asynchronous Programming Overview

In asynchronous programming, one operation does not block the execution of another operation; this is a way of managing concurrency in programming. When waiting for an action to finish could waste processor time that could be utilized for other tasks, this approach comes in handy, especially in I/O-bound and high-latency procedures.

What is Asynchronous Programming?

Asynchronous programming involves executing operations in non-blocking fashion. Unlike synchronous programming, where code is executed sequentially and each line must wait for the previous line to finish before executing, asynchronous code allows a program to handle multiple operations by initiating an operation and moving on to another one before the first has finished.

Asynchronous Programming for Backend Development

Backend systems often deal with operations that can delay the execution of your code, such as database queries, file I/O operations, or requests to other web services. In traditional synchronous programming, the server waits for each of these operations to complete before moving on to the next one. This can lead to inefficient use of resources and poor performance, especially under high load conditions where many requests are handled simultaneously.

Asynchronous programming addresses this by allowing the server to handle other tasks while waiting for I/O operations to complete. This increases the efficiency and responsiveness of the application, allowing it to serve more users without adding additional hardware.

Asynchronous Programming Use Cases

Web Servers

Asynchronous servers are extremely effective for handling web requests. They can manage thousands of connections, making them ideal for real-time web applications. For example, Node.js, initially built on the V8 JavaScript engine, was designed with non-blocking, event-driven architecture to handle numerous simultaneous connections efficiently.

Data Processing

Asynchronous programming can be used to speed up data processing tasks. For instance, when processing large amounts of data from a database or an API, asynchronous methods can fetch and process data in parallel rather than waiting for each query or API call to complete sequentially.

Real-time Applications

Applications like chat apps, live notifications, or real-time data dashboards benefit significantly from asynchronous programming. For example, a chat application can handle sending and receiving messages without interrupting the user interface, providing a smooth and responsive experience.

Microservices Architecture

In a microservices architecture, different services might need to communicate with each other over HTTP. Asynchronous HTTP requests allow these services to operate independently without waiting on responses from each other, thereby improving overall system performance.

How Asynchronous Programming Works?

In Python, asynchronous programming is typically achieved using the **asyncio** library, which provides the framework for running asynchronous tasks and handling callbacks.

Following is a brief overview of how it's structured:

Event Loop

At the heart of **asyncio** is the event loop, which is responsible for managing and distributing the execution of different tasks. It keeps track of all the running tasks and executes them when they are ready, managing their states in non-blocking fashion.

Coroutines

A Coroutine is a function that can pause its execution before reaching return, and it can indirectly pass control to other coroutines for a while. Coroutines are declared with the **async def** keywords, and their execution is paused at **await** expressions.

Futures and Tasks

Futures are objects that link a callback to the outcome of a function. In **asyncio**, tasks are a subtype of Futures that are used to schedule coroutines concurrently. When a coroutine is wrapped into a Task with functions like **asyncio.create_task()**, the event loop can take care of managing its execution.

Sample Program: Asynchronous Execution

Following is a simple example to illustrate asynchronous execution in Python:

```python
import asyncio


async def main():
 print('Hello')
 await asyncio.sleep(1)
 print('World')
```

```
# Run the asynchronous function

asyncio.run(main())
```

In the above code, **asyncio.run(main())** starts running the main coroutine and schedules its execution. The **await asyncio.sleep(1)** statement pauses the coroutine, allowing the event loop to run other tasks (if there were any) during the 1-second sleep, and then resumes it.

Improved application responsiveness and performance, as well as optimized resource consumption (particularly for I/O-bound tasks), are all possible outcomes of this capability. Knowing how to use Python's asyncio package to implement asynchronous operations is now a must-have ability for modern backend engineers.

Asyncio Basics

The **asyncio** library in Python is designed to provide a framework for writing concurrent code using the **async** and **await** syntax. This library is essential for asynchronous programming in Python, allowing you to perform various asynchronous operations without blocking the main execution thread. Knowing the basics of **asyncio**, and the key syntax of **async** and **await**, helps significantly to enhance the efficiency of our Python applications, especially when it comes to I/O-bound and high-concurrency situations.

'async' Syntax

The **async** keyword is used to declare a function as a coroutine, which is a type of function that can suspend its execution before reaching return, and it can indirectly pass control to other coroutines for a while.

```
async def fetch_data():
  # Imaginary function that fetches data asynchronously
  data = await some_async_operation()
  return data
```

'await' Syntax

The **await** keyword is used within an **async** function to pause the execution of the coroutine until the awaited task is complete. **await** can only be used inside **async** functions. This allows other tasks to run in the meantime, making efficient use of the event loop.

```python
async def process_data():
 data = await fetch_data()
 print("Data processed:", data)
```

Structure of Asyncio Program

Given below is a basic structure of an **asyncio** program:

```python
import asyncio


async def main():
 print('Start')
 await asyncio.sleep(1) # Simulates an asynchronous I/O operation
 print('Finish')


asyncio.run(main())
```

In the above sample program, **asyncio.run(main())** is used to execute the **main** coroutine, which manages other **async** functions and tasks.

Sample Program: Integrate Asyncio in University Application

Let us integrate **asyncio** into the university management system, particularly focusing on a simulated scenario where asynchronous operations are required, such as fetching student information and processing enrollment asynchronously.

```python
import asyncio
```

```python
# Simulated database call
async def get_student(student_id):
 print(f"Fetching data for student {student_id}")
 await asyncio.sleep(2) # Simulate database response time
 return {"id": student_id, "name": "John Doe"}


# Simulated database call
async def enroll_student_in_course(student, course_id):
 print(f"Enrolling {student['name']} in course
{course_id}")
 await asyncio.sleep(1) # Simulate enrollment processing
time
 return True


# Main coroutine that orchestrates other coroutines
async def main():
 student_id = 123
 course_id = 101


 # Fetch student information
 student = await get_student(student_id)


 # Enroll student in course
```

```
enrolled = await enroll_student_in_course(student,
course_id)

if enrolled:

print(f"{student['name']} has been enrolled in course
{course_id}")


# Run the main coroutine

asyncio.run(main())
```

In the above sample program,

- Fetching Student Data: **get_student** simulates fetching student data from a database. It's an asynchronous function that waits for two seconds to mimic a database operation.

- Enrolling in a Course: **enroll_student_in_course** simulates enrolling a student in a course. It waits for one second to mimic the process time.

- Orchestration: The **main** coroutine orchestrates these tasks. It waits for the student data to be fetched and then proceeds to enroll the student in a course.

Python projects, particularly those that are I/O-bound or need to handle high concurrency, can benefit significantly from learning the fundamentals of asyncio and incorporating it into their applications. A competence in asynchronous programming in Python is priceless in today's software development since it allows you to produce efficient and comprehensible code utilizing the async and await modules.

Developing Asynchronous Web Applications

When it comes to asynchronous programming, FastAPI's major selling point is its built-in ability to handle asynchronous routes. The ability to explicitly use async and await in endpoint implementations significantly improves the efficiency of operations connected to I/O.

Sample Program: Asynchronous University Application

We shall now enhance the university management system with an asynchronous web server that can handle student data retrieval and course enrollment without blocking the server's responsiveness.

Setup and Installation

First, ensure you have FastAPI and an ASGI server, **uvicorn**, installed:

```
pip install fastapi uvicorn
```

Defining Asynchronous Endpoints

We'll create a simple FastAPI application that includes asynchronous endpoints for fetching student details and enrolling students in courses.

```python
from fastapi import FastAPI, HTTPException

import asyncio


app = FastAPI()


# Mock database operations
async def get_student_db(student_id):
  await asyncio.sleep(1) # Simulate a database operation
  return {"id": student_id, "name": "John Doe"}


async def enroll_student_db(student_id, course_id):
  await asyncio.sleep(1) # Simulate a database operation
  return {"student_id": student_id, "course_id":
course_id}


@app.get("/students/{student_id}")
async def get_student(student_id: int):
  student = await get_student_db(student_id)
```

```python
    if not student:
        raise HTTPException(status_code=404, detail="Student not found")
    return student


@app.post("/enroll/{student_id}/{course_id}")
async def enroll_student(student_id: int, course_id: int):
    enrollment = await enroll_student_db(student_id, course_id)
    if not enrollment:
        raise HTTPException(status_code=404, detail="Enrollment failed")
    return {"message": "Student enrolled successfully", "enrollment": enrollment}


if __name__ == "__main__":
    import uvicorn
    uvicorn.run(app, host="127.0.0.1", port=8000)
```

In the above sample program,

- **get_student_db** and **enroll_student_db** are simulated asynchronous functions that mimic database operations. These functions use **asyncio.sleep** to simulate the latency of database operations.

- The **get_student** endpoint fetches student details asynchronously without blocking other requests. Similarly, the **enroll_student** endpoint handles enrolling a student in a course asynchronously.

- The application is run with Uvicorn, an ASGI server, which is designed to support asynchronous code execution. It allows FastAPI to handle multiple requests concurrently, significantly improving performance under load.

- Using **asyncio** with FastAPI is especially effective for applications where operations such as accessing student information and processing enrollments can benefit from non-blocking I/O.

Asynchronous Database Access

Understanding Asynchronous Database Access

Traditional synchronous database operations block the execution thread until the database server responds. This can degrade performance, especially under heavy loads where multiple users are performing database operations simultaneously. Asynchronous database access addresses this issue by allowing the execution to continue with other tasks while waiting for the database operations to complete.

While many traditional Python database drivers do not support asyncio out of the box, there are several libraries designed to work with asyncio for asynchronous database communication. For SQL databases, **aiomysql** (for MySQL) and **aiopg** (for PostgreSQL) provide asyncio-compatible interfaces. For this example, assuming we're using a PostgreSQL database, we will use **aiopg**.

Setup and Installation

First, you need to install the required package, **aiopg**, which is an asyncio-compatible library for PostgreSQL:

```
pip install aiopg
```

Integrating Asynchronous Database Operations in FastAPI

To demonstrate asynchronous database operations, let's refactor the previous example of the university application to use **aiopg** for fetching student details and handling enrollments.

Configuration

First, set up the database connection using **aiopg**. It's common to handle database connection pooling and session management at the application startup and shutdown events in FastAPI:

```
from fastapi import FastAPI
```

```python
import aiopg


app = FastAPI()


dsn = 'dbname=mydatabase user=myuser password=mypassword host=127.0.0.1'
db_pool = None


@app.on_event("startup")
async def startup():
 global db_pool
 db_pool = await aiopg.create_pool(dsn)


@app.on_event("shutdown")
async def shutdown():
 global db_pool
 if db_pool:
 db_pool.close()
 await db_pool.wait_closed()
```

Asynchronous Database Functions

With the connection pool configured, you can now write asynchronous functions to interact with the database. These functions will use connections from the pool and execute SQL queries asynchronously.

```python
async def get_student_db(student_id):
```

```python
async with db_pool.acquire() as connection:
    async with connection.cursor() as cursor:
        await cursor.execute("SELECT * FROM students WHERE id = %s", (student_id,))
        student_record = await cursor.fetchone()
        if student_record:
            return {
                "id": student_record[0],
                "name": student_record[1],
                "email": student_record[2]
            }
        return None


async def enroll_student_db(student_id, course_id):
    async with db_pool.acquire() as connection:
        async with connection.cursor() as cursor:
            await cursor.execute(
                "INSERT INTO enrollments (student_id, course_id) VALUES (%s, %s)",
                (student_id, course_id)
            )
            await connection.commit()
    return True
```

Modify the FastAPI route handlers to utilize these asynchronous database functions:

```python
@app.get("/students/{student_id}")

async def get_student(student_id: int):

 student = await get_student_db(student_id)

 if not student:

 raise HTTPException(status_code=404, detail="Student not found")

 return student
```

```python
@app.post("/enroll/{student_id}/{course_id}")

async def enroll_student(student_id: int, course_id: int):

 success = await enroll_student_db(student_id, course_id)

 if not success:

 raise HTTPException(status_code=500, detail="Enrollment failed")

 return {"message": "Student enrolled successfully"}
```

Since this method avoids blocking the web server while waiting for database operations to finish, it is especially useful in settings where the application has to handle a large number of concurrent database actions.

Implementing Websockets

Understanding WebSockets

WebSockets provide a way for two-way communication between a client and a server over a single, long-lived connection. Unlike HTTP requests, which are stateless and closed after a response is sent, WebSocket connections remain open, allowing real-time data transfer and immediate interactions. This makes WebSockets particularly suitable for applications that require constant data updates or real-time interaction, such as live messaging apps, real-time feeds, or interactive games.

WebSockets enable messages to be sent and received between a browser and a server without reopening the connection, reducing both latency and overhead. This continuous connection state is initiated by an HTTP handshake followed by a protocol upgrade from HTTP to WebSocket.

Implementing WebSockets in FastAPI

FastAPI provides built-in support for WebSockets, making it straightforward to implement real-time communication features. For the university application scenario, let's consider implementing a WebSocket that allows real-time updates on course enrollment to admins or students.

Setup and Basic WebSocket Endpoint

To begin, we'll set up a basic WebSocket endpoint using FastAPI that will listen for incoming connections and send back messages to the client.

Install FastAPI and Uvicorn

If not already installed, make sure you have FastAPI and Uvicorn, an ASGI server, installed to run your application.

```
pip install fastapi uvicorn
```

Define WebSocket Endpoint

Create a new FastAPI app and define a WebSocket route that will handle incoming WebSocket connections.

```
from fastapi import FastAPI, WebSocket,
WebSocketDisconnect


app = FastAPI()


@app.websocket("/ws")

async def websocket_endpoint(websocket: WebSocket):
```

```
await websocket.accept()

try:

while True:

data = await websocket.receive_text()

await websocket.send_text(f"Message received: {data}")

except WebSocketDisconnect:

print("Client disconnected")
```

This endpoint establishes a WebSocket connection at the route **/ws**. The **websocket.accept()** method accepts the incoming connection. The server then enters a loop where it listens for messages (**receive_text()**) and echoes each received message back to the client (**send_text()**).

Real-Time Course Enrollment Updates

To demonstrate a practical application, let's enhance the WebSocket to notify connected clients whenever a new enrollment is processed. This could be useful for real-time updates in an admin dashboard.

Store WebSocket Connections

Manage multiple active WebSocket connections by storing them, typically in a list or a more complex manager class, which handles connections and broadcasts messages to all connected clients.

```
class ConnectionManager:

 def __init__(self):

 self.active_connections: List[WebSocket] = []


 async def connect(self, websocket: WebSocket):

 await websocket.accept()

 self.active_connections.append(websocket)
```

```python
def disconnect(self, websocket: WebSocket):
    self.active_connections.remove(websocket)

async def broadcast(self, message: str):
    for connection in self.active_connections:
        await connection.send_text(message)

manager = ConnectionManager()

@app.websocket("/ws")
async def websocket_endpoint(websocket: WebSocket):
    await manager.connect(websocket)
    try:
        while True:
            data = await websocket.receive_text()
            await manager.broadcast(f"New enrollment: {data}")
    except WebSocketDisconnect:
        manager.disconnect(websocket)
        print("Client disconnected")
```

Integrate with Enrollment Process

Modify the enrollment endpoint to broadcast a message to all connected WebSocket clients whenever a new student enrolls in a course.

```python
@app.post("/enroll/{student_id}/{course_id}")
async def enroll_student(student_id: int, course_id:
int):
 # Assume enrollment logic here
 success = await enroll_student_db(student_id, course_id)
 if success:
 await manager.broadcast(f"Student {student_id} enrolled
in course {course_id}")
 return {"message": "Student enrolled successfully"}
 raise HTTPException(status_code=500, detail="Enrollment
failed")
```

A more engaging and responsive administrative dashboard is possible with the help of WebSockets, which the university app makes use of to update clients in real-time on course enrollments.

Async Best Practices and Patterns

Error Handling in Asynchronous Code

In asynchronous programming, especially when using frameworks like FastAPI and libraries like **asyncio**, adhering to certain practices and patterns can significantly enhance the robustness, maintainability, and performance of your applications. Asynchronous operations often introduce complexity in error handling due to the non-blocking nature and the potential chaining of operations. Handling errors properly ensures that your application remains robust and user-friendly.

Sample Program: Graceful Handling of Database Errors

Consider implementing error handling for database operations that might fail due to connection issues or data inconsistencies.

```python
async def get_student(student_id: int):
 try:
```

```
student = await database.fetch_student(student_id)

return student

except ConnectionError:

# Handle connection-specific errors

logger.error("Failed to connect to the database.")

raise HTTPException(status_code=500, detail="Database
connection failed")

except Exception as e:

# Handle other kinds of errors

logger.error(f"An error occurred: {e}")

raise HTTPException(status_code=500, detail="An internal
error occurred")
```

Managing Concurrency and Task Cancellation

Handling concurrency properly is crucial in asynchronous applications to prevent memory leaks and ensure that resources are managed efficiently. Task cancellation is a part of this, allowing for stopping potentially long-running or hung tasks programmatically.

Sample Program: Canceling Stale Database Queries

When performing a potentially long-running query, you might want to implement a timeout or cancellation feature.

```
from asyncio import TimeoutError


async def fetch_data_with_timeout():
  try:

  return await
asyncio.wait_for(database.fetch_large_data_set(),
timeout=10.0)
```

```
except TimeoutError:

 logger.warning("The database query was cancelled due to
a timeout.")

 return None
```

Use of Context Managers for Resource Management

Context managers are incredibly useful in asynchronous programming for managing resources like database connections or files. They ensure that resources are properly cleaned up after their use, preventing resource leakage.

Sample Program: Asynchronous Context Manager for Database Connection

```
from contextlib import asynccontextmanager


@asynccontextmanager
async def get_database_connection():
 conn = await database.connect()
 try:
 yield conn
 finally:
 await conn.close()


async def use_database():
 async with get_database_connection() as conn:
 result = await conn.execute("SELECT * FROM students")
 data = await result.fetchall()
 return data
```

Decoupling and Modularization

In asynchronous programming, decoupling components and modularizing the code can help manage complexity, especially as applications scale.

Sample Program: Modularizing WebSocket Handling

Instead of handling WebSocket connections directly within endpoint functions, you can modularize the WebSocket management into a separate module or class.

```python
class WebSocketManager:
  def __init__(self):
  self.active_connections = []


  async def connect(self, websocket):
  await websocket.accept()
  self.active_connections.append(websocket)


  async def broadcast(self, message):
  for websocket in self.active_connections:
  await websocket.send_text(message)


  async def disconnect(self, websocket):
  self.active_connections.remove(websocket)


# Usage in FastAPI routes
websocket_manager = WebSocketManager()
```

```
@app.websocket("/ws/{user_id}")

async def websocket_endpoint(websocket: WebSocket,
user_id: int):

 await websocket_manager.connect(websocket)

 try:

 while True:

 data = await websocket.receive_text()

 await websocket_manager.broadcast(f"User {user_id} sent:
{data}")

 except WebSocketDisconnect:

 websocket_manager.disconnect(websocket)
```

Applying these patterns and techniques within the university management application guarantees that the application's asynchronous components are efficient, manageable, and robust. Your system can make full use of asynchronous programming to provide a dependable and responsive user experience if you handle mistakes graciously, manage resources effectively, and modularize the components.

Debugging Asynchronous Applications

The concurrent operation of asynchronous applications makes debugging them a common challenge. Conventional methods of debugging may be ineffective when problems do not follow a predictable or linear pattern. Our FastAPI-built university management software is a complex system, but with the correct tools and methods, we were able to successfully identify and fix problems with asynchronous code.

Debugging Tools and Techniques

Sample Program: Adding Detailed Logging

In asynchronous applications, logging is vital because it provides insights into what the application is doing at any point in time. It can help trace the flow of execution and understand how data is being processed.

```python
import logging

from fastapi import FastAPI, WebSocket,
WebSocketDisconnect

import asyncio


logging.basicConfig(level=logging.INFO)
logger = logging.getLogger(__name__)


app = FastAPI()


@app.websocket("/ws")
async def websocket_endpoint(websocket: WebSocket):
 await websocket.accept()
 try:
 while True:
 data = await websocket.receive_text()
 logger.info(f"Received data: {data}")
 await websocket.send_text(f"Message received: {data}")
 logger.info(f"Sent confirmation to client.")
 except WebSocketDisconnect:
 logger.warning(f"WebSocket disconnected.")
```

In this setup, logs provide a clear trace of when data is received and when responses are sent back, as well as when a client disconnects unexpectedly.

Sample Program: Using Print Statements for Immediate Feedback

While not the most sophisticated method, print statements (or logging at a debug level) can be strategically placed to output internal state information or variable values in development environments, which can be extremely useful for quick checks.

```python
@app.post("/enroll/{student_id}/{course_id}")

async def enroll_student(student_id: int, course_id: int):

  print(f"Attempting to enroll student {student_id} in course {course_id}")

  enrollment = await enroll_student_db(student_id, course_id)

  if not enrollment:

  print("Enrollment failed")

  raise HTTPException(status_code=500, detail="Enrollment failed")

  print("Enrollment succeeded")

  return {"message": "Student enrolled successfully"}
```

This method can provide immediate and clear feedback on what is happening in the function at runtime.

Sample Program: Enabling asyncio Debug Mode

The asyncio library provides a debug mode that can be very helpful for catching common issues such as tasks that are not awaited, slow tasks, and tasks that are cancelled but never awaited. Debug mode logs a lot of additional information about the internal state of the asyncio event loop.

```python
import os


# Set the environment variable before running the application

os.environ['PYTHONASYNCIODEBUG'] = '1'
```

```
# Alternatively, you can set the debug mode
programmatically

import asyncio


asyncio.get_event_loop().set_debug(True)
```

Asynchronous application debugging makes use of both standard debugging techniques and tools designed for this type of execution. The debug mode in asyncio, together with thorough logging, integrated development environment (IDE) debugging tools, simple print statements, and other techniques, allows developers to effectively trace and diagnose errors in asynchronous applications.

Summary

This chapter covered a lot of ground when it came to asynchronous programming in Python, with an emphasis on different parts that let programmers create efficient and responsive apps. An introduction to asynchronous programming outlining its key features and how it differs from conventional synchronous programming was the first part of the chapter. Next, we dove into the fundamentals of asyncio to write concurrent programs using the async/await syntax. A solid groundwork for dealing with asynchronous tasks was laid out by the practical examples that showed how to include fundamental asynchronous functions into a web application.

The following section demonstrated how to utilize FastAPI to create non-blocking web services, and it also taught the development of asynchronous web applications. Here you can find examples of real-world applications that manage web sockets for real-time communication and process data interactions in real-time.

Additionally, asynchronous database access became the center of attention. We covered methods to improve the application's responsiveness and performance under load by integrating asyncio-compatible database drivers and running non-blocking database operations.

Also taught were concurrency and parallelism, with an emphasis on how asyncio makes use of both to improve the runtime of asynchronous programs. There was also an section of how to construct websockets, which allowed for real-time, two-way communication between servers and clients.

Finally, the chapter covered debugging strategies that are asynchronously optimized, as well as best practices and patterns for creating asynchronous code that is both clean and easy to maintain.

In order to keep complicated asynchronous applications running smoothly and effectively, it is important to be familiar with appropriate error handling, resource management, and debugging techniques, all of which are covered in these sections.

CHAPTER 7: USER MANAGEMENT AND SECURITY

Introduction

In this chapter, we will explore the fundamentals of web application security, specifically looking at user management and data security. Starting with user authentication system design, the chapter delves into how these systems should be structured to properly handle user identities while maintaining security standards. You will find an overview of the ideas and processes that support user authentication, as well as a rundown of the necessary steps and any obstacles you may face.

The next section of the chapter delves into the use of OAuth and JSON Web Tokens (JWT) to control who has access to what resources. These protocols offer ways to safely and efficiently manage user rights and access controls; they are essential to contemporary web security and are extensively utilized for authorization in web applications. Role-Based Access Control (RBAC) is the next topic of learning. It is a way to limit system access to authorized users according to their role in an organization. Here we'll go over the ins and outs of RBAC system design and implementation, which will help you fine-tune your security policies and provide users the access they need.

Another vital topic covered in this chapter is the security of REST APIs. Ensuring the security of data exchanged between clients and servers is the main focus, with a focus on strategies to protect APIs from typical vulnerabilities and attacks. In addition, we take a look at user session management, covering tactics for safely handling user sessions, such as best practices for session creation, maintenance, and expiration that prevent hijacking and other security risks.

Last but not least, we have a look at two-factor authentication (2FA), which adds another safeguard by necessitating two kinds of verification. In order to strengthen security, this section shows how to incorporate two-factor authentication into current authentication systems.

When taken as a whole, these topics offer a thorough framework for creating user management systems that are both secure and strong, protecting the users and the data they access. Anyone working in development or security who wants to make their web apps more secure must have this groundwork.

Designing User Authentication Systems

The security of our university app, like any other app, depends on how well we design our user authentication system. A system like this would check the credentials of anyone attempting to use the platform to make sure they are who they say they are. In this section, we will go into the fundamentals of building a strong user authentication system for the university application, covering all the necessary steps and factors to keep in mind.

Understanding Requirements

The first step in designing an authentication system is to define the specific requirements of the application. For the university app, consider the following needs:

- The app likely needs to support different types of users, such as students, faculty, and administrative staff, each with different access rights.

- Sensitive information, like student grades or faculty salary details, requires higher security measures compared to general information like course descriptions.

- The system must be easy to use to ensure that all users can effectively interact with it without facing barriers.

- As the university grows, the system should be able to handle an increasing number of users and sessions without performance degradation.

- Depending on the location, there may be regulatory requirements regarding the handling and protection of student data (such as FERPA in the U.S.).

Components of a User Authentication System

With the requirements in mind, you can start designing the system by determining the necessary components:

- Database Schema: Design a database to store user credentials securely. Typically, this includes a users table with fields for the user ID, username, password (hashed), email, and perhaps a role identifier.

- Registration Process: Allow new users to register. This usually involves collecting essential information, verifying an email address or mobile number, and securely handling passwords.

- Login Process: Create a secure login mechanism. This includes a form for username and password entry, which should be transmitted over a secure connection (HTTPS).

- Session Management: After authentication, the system should create a session for the user, which is maintained across the website to recognize the user on subsequent requests without them needing to re-authenticate.

- Password Storage: Implement secure password storage practices, such as using a strong hashing algorithm with a salt to protect passwords in your database.

Sample Program: Infusing User Authentication

Following is a simplified outline of implementing the user authentication system in a Python web framework like Flask:

- Setup a Flask App.

```
from flask import Flask, request, session
```

```python
from flask_bcrypt import Bcrypt


app = Flask(__name__)
app.secret_key = 'your_secret_key_here'
bcrypt = Bcrypt(app)
```

- User Registration Endpoint

```python
@app.route('/register', methods=['POST'])
def register():
 username = request.form['username']
 password = request.form['password']
 hashed_password =
bcrypt.generate_password_hash(password).decode('utf-8')
 # Save the username and hashed_password to the database
 return "User registered successfully"
```

- User Login Endpoint

```python
@app.route('/login', methods=['POST'])
def login():
 username = request.form['username']
 password = request.form['password']
 # Fetch the user's hashed password from the database
 user_hashed_password = 'fetched_from_db'
 if bcrypt.check_password_hash(user_hashed_password,
password):
```

```
session['user'] = username

return "Logged in successfully"

else:

return "Invalid credentials", 401
```

While designing each of these components, keep in mind the university app's unique needs for usability and security, and make sure they can scale to satisfy any regulatory requirements.

Implementing OAuth and JWT

These days, no web security solution is complete without OAuth and JSON Web Tokens, which are particularly useful when authenticating and authorizing users across several systems requires an extra layer of security. Let us take a closer look at these technologies and see how we might include them into the backend of our university application.

Introduction to OAuth

OAuth is an open standard for access delegation commonly used as a way for Internet users to grant websites or applications access to their information on other websites but without giving them the passwords. It is designed to work over HTTP and provides tokens instead of credentials to access their data hosted by a given service provider. OAuth is especially useful when trying to provide a secure and efficient way for users to log in using external services (like Google, Facebook, or Twitter) without exposing their password.

Introduction to JSON Web Tokens (JWT)

JWTs are a compact, URL-safe means of representing claims to be transferred between two parties. The claims in a JWT are encoded as a JSON object that is used as the payload of a JSON Web Signature (JWS) structure or as the plaintext of a JSON Web Encryption (JWE) structure, enabling the claims to be digitally signed or integrity protected with a Message Authentication Code (MAC) and/or encrypted.

JWTs are used in authentication and authorization protocols, including OAuth 2.0, because they are JSON-based, more compact, and more straightforward than XML-based SAML tokens.

Sample Program: Implementing OAuth and JWT

The integration of OAuth and JWT into our university application can facilitate secure and scalable user authentication and authorization, particularly for accessing and interacting with third-party services.

Setting up OAuth with Provider

Suppose you want to enable users to log in using their Google accounts. You would start by setting up OAuth credentials with Google:

- Visit the Google Cloud Console.

- Create a new project or select an existing project.

- Navigate to "APIs & Services" > "Credentials".

- Click "Create credentials" and select "OAuth client ID".

- Configure the consent screen and set the application type to web application.

- Add authorized redirect URIs that will handle the response from Google.

You will receive a client ID and a client secret upon creating your credentials. Store these securely.

Integrating OAuth in Application

Use a library like **Authlib** or **Flask-OAuthlib** if you are using Flask:

```
from authlib.integrations.flask_client import OAuth


app = Flask(__name__)
oauth = OAuth(app)


google = oauth.register(
 name='google',
 client_id='YOUR_GOOGLE_CLIENT_ID',
 client_secret='YOUR_GOOGLE_CLIENT_SECRET',

access_token_url='https://accounts.google.com/o/oauth2/token',
 access_token_params=None,
```

```
authorize_url='https://accounts.google.com/o/oauth2/auth'
,
 authorize_params=None,
 api_base_url='https://www.googleapis.com/oauth2/v1/',
 client_kwargs={'scope': 'openid profile email'},
)
```

Implementing JWT for Session Management

Once a user is authenticated using OAuth, you can generate a JWT to manage their session securely:

```python
import jwt
from datetime import datetime, timedelta


def create_token(user_id):
 payload = {
 'exp': datetime.utcnow() + timedelta(days=1), # Token expires in one day
 'iat': datetime.utcnow(), # Token issued at
 'sub': user_id # Subject (whom the token refers to)
 }
 return jwt.encode(payload, 'YOUR_SECRET_KEY', algorithm='HS256')


@app.route('/login/callback')
def login_callback():
```

```
token = google.authorize_access_token()

resp = google.get('userinfo')

user_info = resp.json()

# Create a JWT token after successful OAuth
authentication

jwt_token = create_token(user_info['id'])

return {'jwt_token': jwt_token}
```

With OAuth, students may use their existing Google accounts to access the university app, streamlining the login procedure and improving security (passwords aren't stored directly in your app). The application is further secured by using JWTs to handle client-server sessions and claims after signing in. This ensures that user sessions are managed effectively and securely.

Role-Based Access Control (RBAC)

RBAC is a way for businesses to control who has access to what on their networks and computers depending on their job titles. Applying RBAC is critical for the university app since it guarantees that users (students, teachers, and admins) can only access the data and features that are pertinent to their jobs.

Understanding RBAC's Effectiveness

RBAC is effective because it simplifies managing user permissions. Instead of assigning permissions to each user individually, roles are created for each set of permissions, and users are assigned roles. This makes it easier to manage complex permissions and ensures consistent security policy enforcement across an application.

Sample Program: Implementing RBAC

To demonstrate the implementation of RBAC, let's consider a Python web application using Flask, as it's a common choice for building web applications.

Define Roles and Permissions

First, define what roles exist and what permissions those roles should have. For the university application, you might define roles such as:

1. Student: Can view their course schedules, grades, and enroll in courses.

2. Professor: Can view and manage their courses, grade assignments.

3. Admin: Can manage user accounts, edit all courses, view all student records.

Permissions might look like this:

- **view_grades**

- **edit_courses**

- **view_courses**

- **manage_users**

Setting up the Environment

- Install Flask and Flask-SQLAlchemy for handling the application and database.

```
pip install Flask Flask-SQLAlchemy
```

- Set up the application and the database.

```
from flask import Flask
from flask_sqlalchemy import SQLAlchemy


app = Flask(__name__)
app.config['SQLALCHEMY_DATABASE_URI'] =
'sqlite:///university.db'
db = SQLAlchemy(app)
```

Define User and Role Models

Define SQLAlchemy models for **User**, **Role**, and a helper table for a many-to-many relationship between users and roles.

```
class User(db.Model):
  id = db.Column(db.Integer, primary_key=True)
```

```python
    username = db.Column(db.String(80), unique=True,
nullable=False)

    roles = db.relationship('Role', secondary='user_roles')


class Role(db.Model):
    id = db.Column(db.Integer, primary_key=True)

    name = db.Column(db.String(50), unique=True,
nullable=False)


class UserRoles(db.Model):
    user_id = db.Column(db.Integer,
db.ForeignKey('user.id'), primary_key=True)

    role_id = db.Column(db.Integer,
db.ForeignKey('role.id'), primary_key=True)
```

Populate Roles

Initialize the database and add roles.

```python
with app.app_context():
    db.create_all()

    student_role = Role(name="Student")

    professor_role = Role(name="Professor")

    admin_role = Role(name="Admin")

    db.session.add_all([student_role, professor_role,
admin_role])

    db.session.commit()
```

Assign Roles to Users

When creating a new user, assign roles accordingly.

```
new_user = User(username="john_doe")

new_user.roles.append(student_role)

db.session.add(new_user)

db.session.commit()
```

Enforce Role Checks

Create a simple role checker for routes.

```
from flask import abort


def role_required(*roles):
  def wrapper(fn):
  @wraps(fn)
  def decorated_view(*args, **kwargs):
  if not current_user or not any(role.name in roles for
role in current_user.roles):
  abort(403) # Forbidden access
  return fn(*args, **kwargs)
  return decorated_view
  return wrapper


@app.route('/view_grades')

@role_required('Student', 'Professor')
```

```
def view_grades():

 return "Grades"
```

In the above sample program, we see how user roles are created and then used to implement access control. This method makes it easy for the program to handle user permissions and make sure that only authorized users can do actions, which keeps the data secure and private.

Securing REST APIs

Why Security for REST API?

REST APIs often act as the interface to a web server's data and functionality, making them a prime target for attacks. Without proper security, APIs can expose sensitive data, allow unauthorized access, and potentially lead to service disruption. Safeguarding REST APIs is essential for keeping client-server data private, intact, and accessible to authorized users only. This method employs a range of techniques to safeguard the API from typical attack vectors and mitigate vulnerabilities, including Man-in-the-Middle (MitM) attacks, SQL injection, Cross-Site Scripting (XSS), and others.

Strategies for Securing REST APIs

Use HTTPS

The first and simplest step is ensuring all communications between your client and server are encrypted using HTTPS. This prevents intercepting and reading your data in transit by malicious parties.

```
# Ensure Flask app enforces HTTPS

from flask import Flask, request, jsonify, redirect


app = Flask(__name__)


@app.before_request

def before_request():
```

```
if not request.is_secure:

url = request.url.replace('http://', 'https://', 1)

code = 301

return redirect(url, code=code)
```

Authentication and Authorization

Both authentication and authorization check that users are legitimate before granting them access to resources. For safe and efficient session management and authentication, use JWTs as below:

```python
import jwt

from flask import request, abort


@app.route('/api/resource')

def get_resource():

  token = request.headers.get('Authorization')

  try:

  payload = jwt.decode(token, "SECRET_KEY",
algorithms=["HS256"])

  except (jwt.DecodeError, jwt.ExpiredSignatureError):

  abort(401) # Unauthorized access

  user_id = payload['sub']

  # Check if user_id has access to this resource

  return jsonify({"data": "Secure data"})
```

Validate and Sanitize Input

To protect your API from SQL injection and other forms of injection attacks, always validate and sanitize user inputs:

```python
from flask import request
from marshmallow import Schema, fields, ValidationError


class ResourceSchema(Schema):
  resource_id = fields.Int(required=True)


@app.route('/api/resource', methods=["POST"])
def create_resource():
  json_input = request.get_json()
  try:
  data = ResourceSchema().load(json_input)
  except ValidationError as err:
  return jsonify(err.messages), 400
  resource_id = data['resource_id']
  # Process the valid `resource_id` safely
  return jsonify({"message": "Resource created"}), 201
```

Implement Rate Limiting

Rate limiting helps prevent abuse and DoS (Denial of Service) attacks by limiting how many requests a user or IP can make in a given amount of time.

```python
from flask_limiter import Limiter
from flask_limiter.util import get_remote_address


limiter = Limiter(
```

```
app,

key_func=get_remote_address,

default_limits=["200 per day", "50 per hour"]

)


@app.route("/api/resource")

@limiter.limit("10 per minute")

def get_resource():

  return jsonify({"data": "This is rate-limited"})
```

These above tactics provide a solid strategy to secure your REST API from different types of security risks, which in turn protects your data and your users.

User Session Management

In order to keep online applications secure, user session management is essential, especially when dealing with stateless HTTP protocols and user interactions. From the moment a user logs in to the moment they log out, secure session management procedures safeguard user data by preventing unauthorized access and session hijacking.

Core Concepts

- Session Creation: When a user logs in successfully, the server creates a session, which is typically represented by a session identifier (session ID). This session ID must be unique and unpredictable to prevent potential attackers from guessing or forging a valid session ID.

- Session Storage: The session data can be stored either on the client-side (in cookies) or on the server-side (in a database or in-memory storage). Each approach has its implications for performance and security.

- Session Expiration: Sessions should have a defined lifespan after which they expire automatically. This prevents old sessions from being used indefinitely, which can be a security risk.

- Session Maintenance: During a session, it is important to manage and update session details as needed while ensuring that the session remains secure against threats like fixation or hijacking.

Implementing Secure Session Management

Using Flask, you can implement the above aspects of session management:

Session Creation and Handling

When a user logs in, Flask can handle session creation automatically. Flask's session mechanism signs the cookies to prevent tampering:

```python
from flask import Flask, session, request, redirect, url_for


app = Flask(__name__)

app.secret_key = 'your_secret_key' # Secret key for signing the session cookie


@app.route('/login', methods=['POST'])

def login():

 username = request.form['username']

 password = request.form['password']

 user = validate_user(username, password)

 if user:

 session['user_id'] = user.id # Store user identifier in session

 return redirect(url_for('dashboard'))

 return 'Invalid username or password', 401
```

Session Storage

Sessions in Flask are stored in client-side cookies by default. For better security, you can configure Flask to store session data on the server-side using extensions like Flask-Session:

```
from flask_session import Session


app.config['SESSION_TYPE'] = 'filesystem' # Store
sessions on the filesystem

Session(app)
```

This configuration enhances security by storing the actual session data server-side and only sending a session ID to the client, reducing the risk of client-side tampering.

Session Expiration

Sessions should be configured to expire after a certain period of inactivity or after a fixed time span:

```
from datetime import timedelta


app.config['PERMANENT_SESSION_LIFETIME'] =
timedelta(hours=1) # Expires after 1 hour
```

This setting ensures that user sessions do not remain active indefinitely, which can prevent the risk of session hijacking, especially on public or shared computers.

Session Maintenance and Security

During the user's session, certain practices help maintain security:

- Regenerate the session ID upon authentication or when the user's role changes to prevent session fixation attacks.

```
@app.route('/login', methods=['POST'])

def login():

  # Assume user is validated
```

```
session.regenerate() # Regenerate session ID

return 'Logged in successfully'
```

- Ensure all session cookies are sent over HTTPS to protect them from being intercepted by attackers.

```
app.config['SESSION_COOKIE_SECURE'] = True
```

- Configure the session cookies to be HttpOnly and set the SameSite attribute to prevent cross-site scripting (XSS) and cross-site request forgery (CSRF).

```
app.config['SESSION_COOKIE_HTTPONLY'] = True

app.config['SESSION_COOKIE_SAMESITE'] = 'Lax'
```

Both the user's data and the application's integrity are protected when secure session management procedures are implemented. These methods help prevent typical vulnerabilities such as session hijacking and fixation.

Implementing Two-Factor Authentication

Understanding Two-Factor Authentication

Two-Factor Authentication, or 2FA, is a security measure that asks for two separate pieces of information from the user in order to authenticate their identity, which significantly increases your application's protection. This method ensures that user accounts are protected in the event that a single factor, such as a password, is compromised. Because there are so many different types of users and roles in the university application system, two-factor authentication (2FA) is a good way to keep critical information and access protected.

Two-factor authentication typically combines something the user knows (like a password) with something the user has (like a smartphone app that generates a time-based code) or something the user has (like a fingerprint). For the university application, we'll focus on a commonly used approach involving a password and a Time-based One-Time Password (TOTP) generated by an app like Google Authenticator or Authy.

Steps to Implement 2FA

Generating Secret Key for User

When a user opts to enable 2FA, generate a secret key that will be used to generate TOTPs. This key must be stored securely in the user's profile in the database.

```python
import pyotp


def generate_secret():
 return pyotp.random_base32()


# Assume we have a function to save this to a user's profile
def setup_2fa(user_id):
 secret = generate_secret()
 save_secret_to_user_profile(user_id, secret)
 return secret
```

Linking Secret Key with Authenticator App

The secret key needs to be entered into a TOTP-generating app. This is often facilitated by showing a QR code to the user, which they can scan with the app.

```python
import pyotp


def get_totp_uri(secret, user_email):
 totp = pyotp.TOTP(secret)
 return totp.provisioning_uri(user_email,
issuer_name="UniversityApp")
```

Verifying TOTP during Login

When a user logs in with their username and password, prompt them to enter the code from their TOTP app. Then, verify this code using the secret stored in their profile.

```python
def verify_totp(token, user_id):
  user_secret = get_secret_from_user_profile(user_id)
  totp = pyotp.TOTP(user_secret)
  return totp.verify(token)
```

Integrating 2FA into Login Process

Modify the login process to include a second step for 2FA verification after the initial password check is successful.

```python
from flask import request, session


@app.route('/login', methods=['POST'])
def login():
  username = request.form['username']
  password = request.form['password']
  if authenticate(username, password):
  # User is prompted for 2FA token after password
verification
  session['pre_2fa_auth_user_id'] = get_user_id(username)
  return 'Enter 2FA code'
  return 'Login failed', 401


@app.route('/verify_2fa', methods=['POST'])
def verify_2fa():
  token = request.form['token']
  user_id = session.pop('pre_2fa_auth_user_id', None)
```

```
if user_id and verify_totp(token, user_id):

# Successful 2FA verification

session['user_id'] = user_id

return 'Login successful'

return 'Invalid 2FA token', 401
```

Secure secret key generation, user-key linking to a TOTP-generating app, and TOTP code verification during login are all parts of this process. The integration significantly improves the application's security, but it does need careful handling of cryptographic components and user data.

Summary

This chapter detailed the essentials of web application user management and security, with an emphasis on the parts that are most important for keeping user information safe and implementing reliable access controls. Beginning with an overview of the fundamental requirements for efficiently identifying and verifying user credentials, the chapter moved on to the process of designing user authentication systems. For a more in-depth look at modern authentication methods like OAuth and JWT, which are critical for providing safe access to resources without revealing user passwords, this particular section laid the foundation for further practical implementation.

Next, we explored RBAC, a crucial approach for limiting system access according to user roles. Another area of emphasis was the security of REST APIs, with a focus on preventing endpoints from common security threats using measures like input validation, token-based authentication, and HTTPS. Also covered in this chapter were safe ways to store and protect passwords, with an emphasis on using strong hashing and salting algorithms. In order to safeguard against session hijacking and other vulnerabilities, we explored user session management and outlined methods to securely handle user sessions from creation to expiration.

Finally, the idea of implementing two-factor authentication was brought up as a way to boost up security by adding another checkpoint to prevent unauthorized access. To ensure that user data in the university app remains secure and uncompromised, these steps constitute an all-encompassing strategy for user management and security.

CHAPTER 8: DEPLOYING PYTHON BACKEND APPLICATIONS

Introduction

In this chapter, we will go over the essentials of deploying Python backend applications. You will learn about the key tools and techniques that can improve the scalability, security, and performance of your web applications. This chapter begins with a brief introduction to Docker and containers, then goes on to describe how these technologies can encapsulate application environments.

After that, we'll go over how to use Docker for Python apps in particular, showing how to containerize them for better deployment and portability. In the next section, we'll take a look at Kubernetes, a sophisticated platform for container orchestration. It helps applications handle higher loads by automatically scaling and managing multiple containers across server clusters.

In keeping with the previous chapter's goal of integration and automation, this one explores best practices for CI/CD in Python backend applications. Additionally, we go over Nginx's function as a reverse proxy, which is to say, an intermediary for client requests. This can help with things like SSL termination, load balancing, and improving security for Python applications. Next, we'll go over SSL certificates and HTTPS settings, which are vital for protecting sensitive data and keeping end-user trust, and how to secure application data while it's in transit.

In the last section of the chapter, we will cover ways to scale Python applications, making sure they can expand to meet user demand without slowing down.

Docker and Containers Overview

As a lightweight substitute for traditional virtualization, containerization has significantly changed the application deployment and management cycles. Docker is the most well-known and extensively used platform among the containerization tools currently available. With Docker, programmers can create standardized software development units called containers that contain an application and all of its dependencies.

Understanding Containerization

Containerization involves encapsulating an application and its environment—dependencies, configurations, scripts, and binaries—into a container. Unlike virtual machines (VMs) that require their own operating system, containers share the host system's OS kernel but maintain isolated processes, filesystems, and networking. This makes containers much more efficient, easier to manage, and less resource-intensive than traditional VMs.

Role of Docker in Containerization

Docker provides the tools and platform to manage the lifecycle of containers. It has become synonymous with container technology due to its ease of use, extensive tooling, and robust ecosystem. Docker uses a simple syntax that allows you to build, ship, and run containers with a series of straightforward commands.

Following are the key components of a docker:

Dockerfile

A text document that contains all the commands a user could call on the command line to assemble an image. Using **docker build** users can create an automated build that executes several command-line instructions in succession.

Docker Images

An immutable file that is essentially a snapshot of a container. Images serve as the building blocks of Docker. They can be stored in a registry and can be pulled to create containers.

Docker Containers

An instance of a Docker image. A container represents the execution of a single application, process, or service.

Docker Hub/Registry

A service that provides space for Docker users to host and share images. The public Docker Hub, maintained by Docker Inc., hosts thousands of images with applications, services, and utilities pre-packaged.

Docker's Dominance

Docker's dominance can be attributed to several factors:

- Portability: Once a Docker container is created, it can be run on any machine that has Docker installed, regardless of the underlying environment. This eliminates the "it works on my machine" problem.

- Version Control and Reusability: Images can be versioned, stored in a registry, and reused multiple times. Organizations can increase efficiencies by using base images that are maintained and updated with security patches.

- Isolation: Docker ensures that applications running in containers are isolated from each other and from the host system. This isolation promotes security and allows multiple containers to run on the same host without interference.

- Scalability and Microservices: Docker's lightweight nature allows for rapid scaling. Containers can be quickly started and stopped, handling spikes in application demand more gracefully. Docker is conducive to a microservices architecture because it allows each part of an application to be housed in separate containers and scaled independently.

Sample Program: Using Docker

To illustrate how Docker is used, let's consider a simple example of containerizing a Python Flask application as below:

- Create a Dockerfile.

```
# Use an official Python runtime as a parent image

FROM python:3.8-slim


# Set the working directory in the container

WORKDIR /app


# Copy the current directory contents into the container at /app

ADD . /app


# Install any needed packages specified in requirements.txt

RUN pip install --trusted-host pypi.python.org -r requirements.txt


# Make port 80 available to the world outside this container

EXPOSE 80


# Define environment variable

ENV NAME World
```

```
# Run app.py when the container launches
CMD ["python", "app.py"]
```

- Build the Docker Image

```
docker build -t my-python-app .
```

- Run the Docker Container.

```
docker run -p 4000:80 my-python-app
```

In this setup, the Dockerfile defines the environment and steps to run a Python Flask application. The image is built with these specifications, and then a container from this image is run.

Using Docker for Python Applications

Python applications can be easily containerized using Docker. This procedure streamlines deployment, guarantees consistency across environments, and is especially useful for managing dependencies and settings. Now, I'll show you how to containerize the university app we have been working around and how to install Docker in our existing development environment.

Installing Docker

Docker must be installed on your Linux system prior to application containerization.

Follow these below steps:

- Update Your Package Index.

```
sudo apt-get update
```

- Install Packages to Allow apt to Use a Repository Over HTTPS.

```
sudo apt-get install \
 apt-transport-https \
 ca-certificates \
```

```
curl \

gnupg \

lsb-release
```

- Add Docker's Official GPG Key

```
curl -fsSL https://download.docker.com/linux/ubuntu/gpg |
sudo gpg --dearmor -o /usr/share/keyrings/docker-archive-
keyring.gpg
```

- Set Up the Stable Repository

```
echo \
"deb [arch=$(dpkg --print-architecture) signed-
by=/usr/share/keyrings/docker-archive-keyring.gpg]
https://download.docker.com/linux/ubuntu \

$(lsb_release -cs) stable" | sudo tee
/etc/apt/sources.list.d/docker.list > /dev/null
```

- Install Docker Engine

```
sudo apt-get update

sudo apt-get install docker-ce docker-ce-cli
containerd.io
```

- Verify That Docker Is Installed Correctly by running the hello-world image

```
sudo docker run hello-world
```

This above setup ensures Docker is installed and running on your system. The **hello-world** container run is a simple test to verify that Docker can pull and run images.

Containerizing the University Application

Now, let's containerize the university application as per the following steps:

Prepare Application

Ensure the Flask application is ready with all necessary files. For instance, you should have:

- **app.py**: The Flask application file.
- **requirements.txt**: A file listing all the dependencies.

Following is a simple **app.py** for demonstration:

```python
from flask import Flask
app = Flask(__name__)


@app.route('/')
def hello_world():
  return 'Hello, World!'


if __name__ == '__main__':
  app.run(host='0.0.0.0')
```

Create Dockerfile

The Dockerfile contains instructions for building the image.

```dockerfile
# Use an official Python runtime as a parent image
FROM python:3.8-slim


# Set the working directory to /app
WORKDIR /app


# Copy the current directory contents into the container at /app
```

```
COPY . /app


# Install any needed packages specified in
requirements.txt

RUN pip install --no-cache-dir -r requirements.txt


# Make port 5000 available to the world outside this
container

EXPOSE 5000


# Define environment variable

ENV NAME World


# Run app.py when the container launches

CMD ["python", "app.py"]
```

Build Docker Image

Navigate to the directory containing your Dockerfile and run:

```
docker build -t university-app .
```

This command builds the Docker image with the tag **university-app**.

Run the Docker Container

To start an instance of your Docker image, run:

```
docker run -p 4000:5000 university-app
```

This command maps port 5000 of the container to port 4000 on your host, allowing you to access the Flask app via **`localhost:4000`** on your browser. This university app is now available in a containerized version that neatly packages all dependencies. You can deploy it to any environment that supports Docker, which simplifies deployment and makes your application more scalable and reliable.

Kubernetes for Application Orchestration

Kubernetes, or K8s for short, is a free and open-source platform for managing and automating the process of deploying and scaling containerized applications. It organizes the application's containers into logical units for better discovery and management. Kubernetes is significant at orchestrating complicated applications, especially ones that need to be deployed across multiple environments, scalable, and have high availability.

Understanding Kubernetes

Kubernetes provides a platform to schedule and run containers on clusters of physical or virtual machines. It abstracts away the underlying infrastructure, making the deployment of applications seamless and scalable.

Key features include:

- Pods: The smallest deployable units created and managed by Kubernetes, usually consisting of one or more containers that share storage/network resources.

- Nodes: A node may be a VM or physical machine, depending on the cluster. Each node hosts multiple pods.

- Services: An abstraction which defines a logical set of Pods and a policy by which to access them - this might include a service discovery mechanism handled by Kubernetes.

- Deployment: Manages the deployment and scaling of a set of Pods, and provides updates to the application's containers.

Installing and Configuring Kubernetes

For development purposes, especially for our university application, Minikube is a significant tool that lets us run Kubernetes locally. Minikube runs a single-node Kubernetes cluster inside a VM on your laptop.

Install Minikube

First, ensure that Docker is installed as Minikube requires it to run containers. Then install Minikube as below:

```
curl -LO
https://storage.googleapis.com/minikube/releases/latest/m
inikube-linux-amd64
```

```
sudo install minikube-linux-amd64 /usr/local/bin/minikube
```

Start Minikube

```
minikube start
```

This above command starts a single-node Kubernetes cluster. You can verify the status with **minikube status**.

Install kubectl

kubectl is the command line tool used to interact with Kubernetes. Install it by following:

```
curl -LO "https://dl.k8s.io/release/$(curl -L -s
https://dl.k8s.io/release/stable.txt)/bin/linux/amd64/kub
ectl"
```

```
chmod +x kubectl
```

```
sudo mv kubectl /usr/local/bin/
```

Deploying University App on Kubernetes

Now, let's deploy the Docker container we created for the university application using Kubernetes as per the following stages:

Create Deployment Configuration

Create a **deployment.yaml** file that describes the desired state of your deployment:

```
apiVersion: apps/v1
```

```
kind: Deployment
```

```
metadata:
```

```
  name: university-app-deployment
```

```
spec:
  replicas: 2
  selector:
  matchLabels:
  app: university-app
  template:
  metadata:
  labels:
  app: university-app
  spec:
  containers:
  - name: university-app
  image: university-app:latest
  ports:
  - containerPort: 5000
```

This configuration tells Kubernetes to maintain two replicas of the university app, ensuring high availability.

Deploy the Application

Use **kubectl** to apply your configuration:

```
kubectl apply -f deployment.yaml
```

Expose the Application

To make the university app accessible from outside the Kubernetes virtual network, you need to create a service:

```yaml
apiVersion: v1
kind: Service
metadata:
 name: university-app-service
spec:
 type: LoadBalancer
 ports:
 - port: 80
 targetPort: 5000
 selector:
 app: university-app
```

Apply this configuration as well:

```
kubectl apply -f service.yaml
```

Access the Application

Since Minikube is being used, enable the Minikube service:

```
minikube service university-app-service
```

With this command, your default browser will open the service, allowing you to interact with your deployed application. Kubernetes makes the university app's deployment, scaling, and management easier and more efficient, so it can handle fluctuating loads and possible growth.

CI/CD for Python Backend Applications

Understanding CI/CD

The goal of continuous integration and delivery (CI/CD) is to build high-quality software that is easy to use and adapt to user needs by automating the testing and deployment of code changes on a regular basis. To ensure that integration errors are caught promptly, Continuous Integration runs automated tests at each merge and merges all developers' working copies to a shared mainline multiple times a day. Continuous Deployment takes this a step further by, assumptive of successful test execution, automatically deploying the application to the production environment upon each new release.

For backend applications, especially those built with Python and running in Docker containers like our university app, CI/CD ensures that new features, fixes, and updates are smoothly transitioned from development to production environments without disrupting the service. This is crucial for maintaining the reliability and availability of backend services that must handle potentially thousands or millions of requests.

Implementing CI/CD for University Application

Given the containerized setup of our university application, we can utilize tools such as Jenkins, GitLab CI/CD, or GitHub Actions to implement a robust CI/CD pipeline.

Version Control Setup

Ensure that your codebase is hosted on a version control platform like GitHub, GitLab, or Bitbucket. This platform will be the trigger point for your CI/CD pipeline.

Choose CI/CD Tool

For this example, let's use GitHub Actions, which integrates directly with GitHub repositories.

- Create a GitHub Actions Workflow:
    - Navigate to your GitHub repository.
    - Click on the "Actions" tab and create a new workflow.
    - Use the starter template for Python applications or start from scratch.
- Configure the Workflow File:
    - Create a **.github/workflows/python-app.yml** file and define the following steps:

```
name: Python application CI/CD


on:

 push:

 branches: [ master ]
```

```yaml
  pull_request:
  branches: [ master ]

jobs:
 build:
 runs-on: ubuntu-latest

 steps:
 - uses: actions/checkout@v2
 - name: Set up Python 3.8
 uses: actions/setup-python@v2
 with:
 python-version: 3.8
 - name: Install dependencies
 run: |
 python -m pip install --upgrade pip
 pip install flake8 pytest
 if [ -f requirements.txt ]; then pip install -r requirements.txt; fi
 - name: Lint with flake8
 run: |
 # stop the build if there are Python syntax errors or undefined names
```

```
flake8 . --count --select=E9,F63,F7,F82 --show-source --
statistics

# exit-zero treats all errors as warnings. The GitHub
editor is 127 chars wide

flake8 . --count --exit-zero --max-complexity=10 --max-
line-length=127 --statistics

- name: Test with pytest

run: |

pytest


deploy:

needs: build

runs-on: ubuntu-latest

if: github.ref == 'refs/heads/master' &&
github.event_name == 'push'

steps:

- uses: actions/checkout@v2

- name: Build Docker image

run: docker build . -t university-app:${{ github.sha }}

- name: Push Docker image to Registry

run: |

echo ${{ secrets.DOCKER_PASSWORD }} | docker login -u
${{ secrets.DOCKER_USERNAME }} --password-stdin

docker push university-app:${{ github.sha }}

- name: Deploy to Kubernetes
```

```
run: kubectl set image deployment/university-app
university-app=university-app:${{ github.sha }}

env:

KUBECONFIG: ${{ secrets.KUBECONFIG }}
```

This workflow defines two jobs:

1. Build: This job installs dependencies, runs linting with flake8, and conducts tests using pytest. It ensures that the application builds and passes all tests.

2. Deploy: This job is conditional on pushes to the master branch and depends on the success of the build job. It builds the Docker image, pushes it to a Docker registry, and then updates a Kubernetes deployment to use the new image.

In order to keep backend applications, such as our university app, healthy, fast, and secure, CI/CD is a must. Software can be automatically, quickly, and securely delivered by integrating CI/CD practices, especially in a containerized environment.

Using Nginx as Reverse Proxy

Role of Nginx

Nginx is a high-performance web server that is also widely used as a reverse proxy and load balancer. As a reverse proxy, Nginx can manage incoming traffic and distribute it to various backend servers based on configuration rules, enhancing the scalability, security, and performance of applications.

In the context of a reverse proxy, Nginx acts as an intermediary for requests from clients seeking resources from servers. It intercepts all requests to the server before they reach the application, which can provide several benefits:

- Nginx can distribute incoming network traffic across several backend servers to optimize resource utilization, maximize throughput, reduce response times, and ensure reliability.

- As a reverse proxy, Nginx can also enhance security by functioning as a gateway for servers to the internet. It can perform tasks such as SSL/TLS termination, thus encrypting and decrypting client requests and server responses, thereby offloading these tasks from the application servers.

- Nginx can also cache the content from the server, reducing the number of requests to the application server, which improves the response time for end-users.

Installing and Configuring Nginx

Following is how to install and configure Nginx:

Install Nginx

On Ubuntu or Debian systems, you can install Nginx directly from the package manager:

```
sudo apt update

sudo apt install nginx
```

After installation, you can start the Nginx service and enable it to run on boot with:

```
sudo systemctl start nginx

sudo systemctl enable nginx
```

Configure Nginx as Reverse Proxy

To configure Nginx as a reverse proxy for the university application, you'll need to modify the Nginx configuration files, typically located in **/etc/nginx/sites-available/**. Following is a basic configuration that sets up Nginx as a reverse proxy:

- Create a Configuration File: Create a new file under **/etc/nginx/sites-available/** called **university-app**.

```
sudo nano /etc/nginx/sites-available/university-app
```

- Reverse Proxy Configuration: Add the following configuration to the file:

```
server {
 listen 80;
 server_name university.gitforgits.com;


 location / {
 proxy_pass http://localhost:5000; # Assuming the Flask
app runs on port 5000
```

```
proxy_http_version 1.1;

proxy_set_header Upgrade $http_upgrade;

proxy_set_header Connection 'upgrade';

proxy_set_header Host $host;

proxy_cache_bypass $http_upgrade;

 }

}
```

This configuration tells Nginx to listen for HTTP requests on port 80 for the domain **university.gitforgits.com** and pass those requests to a Flask application running on the same server on port 5000.

- Enable the Configuration: Link the configuration file from **sites-available** to **sites-enabled** to enable it, and then test the configuration for errors:

```
sudo ln -s /etc/nginx/sites-available/university-app
/etc/nginx/sites-enabled/
```

```
sudo nginx -t
```

- If there are no errors reported, restart Nginx to apply the changes:

```
sudo systemctl restart nginx
```

After all this, it will handle requests to **university.gitforgits.com** and forward them to the Flask application running locally on port 5000. Moreover, using Nginx as a reverse proxy adds a layer of abstraction to network interactions with your backend servers. This can provide additional security measures such as IP whitelisting, rate limiting, and handling of CORS (Cross-Origin Resource Sharing) policies.

SSL Certificates and HTTPS Configuration

Understanding SSL/TLS and HTTPS

Internet security and the authentication of websites rely heavily on SSL (Secure Sockets Layer) certificates. Data transmitted between users and the website is encrypted and protected when configuring HTTPS (Hypertext Transfer Protocol Secure) with SSL certificates. This is especially important for web applications that handle sensitive information, such as a university application. Most browsers will display a padlock icon to show that the connection is secure, and websites that use SSL will display "https" in their URLs.

Generating SSL Certificates

For a university application, you'll need a trusted SSL certificate issued by a Certificate Authority (CA). We shall now go through the process using Let's Encrypt, a popular free Certificate Authority, and Certbot, a tool that simplifies obtaining and installing certificates.

Install Certbot

Certbot is an easy-to-use automatic client that fetches and deploys SSL/TLS certificates for your web server. To install Certbot and its Nginx plugin on a Linux server:

```
sudo apt-get update

sudo apt-get install software-properties-common

sudo add-apt-repository ppa:certbot/certbot

sudo apt-get update

sudo apt-get install certbot python3-certbot-nginx
```

Obtaining Certificate

You can run Certbot with the Nginx plugin to automatically obtain and install certificates and configure Nginx to use them:

```
sudo certbot --nginx -d university.gitforgits.com
```

Replace **university.gitforgits.com** with the domain name of your university application. Certbot will modify the Nginx configuration for your domain to use the newly obtained SSL certificate and set up periodic renewal.

Verify SSL Certificate Installation

You can verify that your SSL certificates are installed correctly by accessing your domain via a web browser using **https://**. The browser should indicate that the connection is secure. Alternatively, you can use online tools like SSL Labs' SSL Test to check your website's SSL configuration.

Configuring HTTPS in Nginx

While Certbot automatically configures Nginx to use the SSL certificate, understanding the changes can help you manage your configuration. Following is what a typical SSL configuration snippet looks like in Nginx:

```
server {

 listen 443 ssl http2;

 server_name university.gitforgits.com;


 ssl_certificate
/etc/letsencrypt/live/university.gitforgits.com/fullchain
.pem;

 ssl_certificate_key
/etc/letsencrypt/live/university.gitforgits.com/privkey.p
em;


 ssl_protocols TLSv1.2 TLSv1.3;

 ssl_ciphers 'ECDHE-ECDSA-AES128-GCM-SHA256:ECDHE-RSA-
AES128-GCM-SHA256';

 ssl_prefer_server_ciphers on;

 ssl_session_cache shared:SSL:10m;


 # Add HSTS (HTTP Strict Transport Security)

 add_header Strict-Transport-Security "max-age=31536000"
always;
```

```
location / {

proxy_pass http://localhost:5000;

proxy_set_header Host $host;

proxy_set_header X-Real-IP $remote_addr;

proxy_set_header X-Forwarded-For
$proxy_add_x_forwarded_for;

proxy_set_header X-Forwarded-Proto $scheme;

}

}
```

Not only does Certbot make it easy to set up SSL/TLS certificates for university apps, it also makes them more trustworthy and credible in the eyes of users. Because it works with Nginx, the app can use the strong security features that come with one of the most popular web servers.

Scaling Python Applications

Need for Scaling

To successfully scale Python applications, one must modify the code so that it can handle more users without sacrificing performance. At peak registration times, for example, thousands of users may try to access the system at once, so the university app may have to deal with multiple load scenarios. With scalability, the application can dynamically adjust its resources to efficiently handle such peak loads.

Horizontal vs. Vertical Scaling

Horizontal Scaling (Scaling Out/In)

This involves adding more machines or instances to your pool of resources to handle increased load. It's particularly effective for distributed systems and is well-supported by container orchestration systems like Kubernetes.

Vertical Scaling (Scaling Up/Down)

This method involves adding more power (CPU, RAM) to your existing machines but is limited by the physical capabilities of the hardware. For most web-based applications, horizontal scaling is preferred due to its flexibility and alignment with cloud-based resources.

Implementing Scaling in Kubernetes

Since Kubernetes is already handling our app containerization, we can take advantage of Kubernetes' features to scale our application horizontally. With the help of a feature known as Horizontal Pod Autoscaler (HPA), Kubernetes can dynamically change the amount of running pods according to the system load.

Define Resource Requests and Limits

Before setting up auto scaling, define the resource requests and limits in your deployment configuration. This is crucial for Kubernetes to make informed decisions about when to scale up or down. Then, update your **deployment.yaml** with resource requests and limits as below:

```yaml
apiVersion: apps/v1

kind: Deployment

metadata:

  name: university-app-deployment

spec:

  replicas: 2

  selector:

  matchLabels:

  app: university-app

  template:

  metadata:

  labels:

  app: university-app

  spec:

  containers:
```

```
- name: university-app

image: university-app:latest

resources:

requests:

cpu: "500m"

memory: "256Mi"

limits:

cpu: "1000m"

memory: "512Mi"

ports:

- containerPort: 5000
```

These settings indicate that each instance of the application needs at least 500m CPU and 256Mi memory to run, with a maximum limit of 1000m CPU and 512Mi memory.

Setup Horizontal Pod Autoscaler

Create an HPA resource that targets your deployment. The HPA adjusts the number of pods in a deployment depending on the CPU utilization.

```
kubectl autoscale deployment university-app-deployment --cpu-percent=50 --min=2 --max=10
```

This command tells Kubernetes to maintain a CPU utilization target of 50% for each pod. If the average CPU utilization exceeds this threshold, Kubernetes starts new pods (up to a maximum of 10) to handle the load.

Monitor Scaling

You can monitor the scaling actions taken by Kubernetes using:

```
kubectl get hpa
```

This approach utilizes the elastic nature of cloud resources effectively and ensures that the application remains responsive, regardless of user demand.

Summary

In this chapter, we looked at how to scale Python backend applications, with an emphasis on how to use cutting-edge tools and methodologies for safe and effective application management. Docker and container technology were introduced at the beginning of the chapter, with an emphasis on how Docker streamlines deployment by enclosing applications into containers. This allows for simple version control and rollback while also providing consistency across various environments.

Next, we moved on to Kubernetes, an orchestration platform that efficiently handles these containers. It became clear that Kubernetes was critical for horizontally scaling applications, which means that they can manage increased loads by distributing application instances across a cluster of servers. During registration periods and other times of fluctuating demand, this was especially helpful for the university app's dynamic scaling needs.

The chapter continued with container management and followed it up with CI/CD (Continuous Integration and Continuous Deployment) best practices. Improved efficiency and dependability of production updates are outcomes of these practices' automation of application testing and deployment. By integrating continuous integration and continuous delivery pipelines with tools like GitHub Actions, any changes made to the application are automatically built, tested, and deployed, eliminating the possibility of human error. Also covered was how to use Nginx as a reverse proxy. With Nginx's assistance, client requests are distributed effectively, security is improved, and application performance is enhanced through caching and load balancing.

At the end of the chapter, we covered specific tactics for scaling applications, as well as SSL certificates and HTTPS configuration to safeguard communications. To sum up, the chapter demonstrated how to scale the university application using Kubernetes, providing practical steps for scaling and showing how to achieve automatic scaling to maintain optimal performance regardless of fluctuating demands.

CHAPTER 9:
MICROSERVICES AND CLOUD INTEGRATION

Introduction

This chapter explores the essential deployment, operational, and architectural strategies for modern Python backend applications, as well as the advanced topics of cloud integration and microservices. To begin, the chapter explains how to use Python for microservice design and construction, demonstrating how to partition a large application into smaller, independently deployable services. In addition to improving scalability and maintainability, this method is well-suited to the ever-changing cloud landscape.

Next, we'll go over how to use Docker and Kubernetes to manage these microservices. These tools offer strong solutions for orchestration and containerization, making it easy to manage, scale, and maintain microservices. This chapter delves into the topic of how Kubernetes automates the deployment, scaling, and operations of containerized services, while Docker containers encapsulate the dependencies and environments of microservices.

In this section, we will go over the best ways to use Amazon Web Services (AWS) to host Python applications. You will learn about the services and resources available in the cloud and how they can improve the performance and efficiency of your applications. The idea of serverless architectures is also introduced in the chapter, with a focus on AWS Lambda and how it enables developers to run code independently of servers. For microservices that run infrequently or asynchronously, this model can be a cost-effective option, and it works very well for applications with unpredictable workloads.

Finally, the chapter teaches how to implement gRPC for inter-service communication. The efficient communication between microservices is the focus of this high-performance, open-source framework, which is suitable for polyglot environments due to its support for numerous programming languages. Using the most up-to-date container technologies, cloud deployment strategies, and communication protocols, this chapter teaches readers how to design, build, and manage microservices architectures efficiently. The end result is backend systems that are scalable, robust, and effective.

Designing and Building Microservices with Python

A monolithic application can be decomposed into smaller, independently deployable services through the process of designing and building microservices. The services operate independently and exchange data through simple protocols, most commonly an HTTP resource API. Applications like university systems benefit significantly from this approach because various modules (such as admissions, course management, and student records) can function semi-independently.

Breaking Down Application into Microservices

To transform the university application into a microservices architecture, we need to identify logical modules that can function as independent services.

Let us consider a basic breakdown:

1. Admissions Service: Handles all functionalities related to student applications and admissions.

2. Course Management Service: Manages course offerings, registrations, and instructor assignments.

3. Student Records Service: Maintains student records, including grades and personal information.

4. Authentication Service: Manages user authentication and authorization across all services.

Define Service Boundaries

Each microservice should own its domain logic and data to ensure loose coupling and high cohesion. For instance:

- Admissions Service might own the databases related to application forms and applicant evaluations.

- Course Management Service controls the course catalog and enrollment data.

- Student Records Service manages databases holding student grades and biographical information.

Create Independent Environments

Each service should be able to run independently during both development and deployment. This requires setting up separate development environments, version control repositories, and databases for each service.

Develop APIs for Inter-service Communication

Services need to communicate with each other using APIs. REST is a popular choice for microservices because of its simplicity and how well it integrates with the web.

Following is a sample API endpoint for the Course Management Service:

```
from flask import Flask, jsonify, request

app = Flask(__name__)
```

```python
# Mock database
courses = {
  'CS101': {'title': 'Introduction to Computer Science',
'capacity': 30, 'enrollment': 0}
}


@app.route('/courses/<course_id>', methods=['GET'])
def get_course(course_id):
  course = courses.get(course_id)
  if course:
  return jsonify(course), 200
  else:
  return jsonify({"message": "Course not found"}), 404


@app.route('/courses/<course_id>/enroll',
methods=['POST'])
def enroll_student(course_id):
  course = courses.get(course_id)
  if course and course['enrollment'] < course['capacity']:
  course['enrollment'] += 1
  return jsonify(course), 200
  else:
  return jsonify({"message": "Enrollment failed"}), 400
```

```python
if __name__ == '__main__':
    app.run(port=5002)
```

Dockerize the Services

Each service should be containerized with Docker to ensure that it can run consistently across different environments.

Following is the sample Dockerfile for Course Management Service:

```
FROM python:3.8-slim

WORKDIR /app

COPY . /app

RUN pip install flask

EXPOSE 5002

CMD ["python", "app.py"]

docker build -t course-management-service .

docker run -p 5002:5002 course-management-service
```

The services work separately, but they must be combined in order for the application as a whole to work. Sometimes, an API Gateway will help with this integration by directing requests to the right services. The application's scalability and maintainability are both improved by this modular approach, which also makes development and deployment processes more flexible.

Managing Microservices with Docker and Kubernetes

A strong strategy for containerization and orchestration is necessary for effective microservice management, which involves making sure each microservice is independent, scalable, and maintainable. With the help of Docker and Kubernetes, this kind of management is made possible, enabling the deployment of services as containers that can be dynamically scaled and managed by Kubernetes.

Containerization with Docker

Docker allows each component of your university application's microservices architecture to be packaged into its own container. This encapsulates its dependencies and runtime environment, minimizing conflicts between services and simplifying deployment processes.

Dockerizing each Microservice

For each microservice in the university system (Admissions, Course Management, Student Records, Authentication), you need to create a Dockerfile that specifies how the service is built.

For example, the Dockerfile for the Course Management service might look like this:

```
# Use an official Python runtime as a base image
FROM python:3.8-slim


# Set the working directory in the container
WORKDIR /app


# Copy the current directory contents into the container
at /app
COPY . /app


# Install any needed packages specified in
requirements.txt
RUN pip install --trusted-host pypi.python.org -r
requirements.txt


# Make port 5002 available to the world outside this
container
EXPOSE 5002
```

```
# Define environment variable
ENV NAME World


# Run app.py when the container launches
CMD ["python", "app.py"]
```

Build and run the Docker container using commands similar to the following:

```
docker build -t course-management-service .
docker run -p 5002:5002 course-management-service
```

Orchestrating with Kubernetes

Kubernetes excels at managing such containerized applications, especially in a microservices architecture where high availability, scalability, and service discovery are critical.

Creating Kubernetes Deployments

Each microservice should have its Kubernetes deployment that describes how many replicas of that service should exist, how they are configured, and how updates are rolled out.

Following is an example of a Kubernetes deployment for the Course Management service:

```
apiVersion: apps/v1
kind: Deployment
metadata:
 name: course-management-deployment
spec:
 replicas: 3
 selector:
```

```
matchLabels:

app: course-management

template:

metadata:

labels:

app: course-management

spec:

containers:

- name: course-management

image: course-management-service:latest

ports:

- containerPort: 5002
```

This deployment configures Kubernetes to ensure that three instances of the Course Management service are always running.

Managing Services with Kubernetes Services

To expose the Course Management service within the Kubernetes cluster, define a Kubernetes service:

```
apiVersion: v1

kind: Service

metadata:

  name: course-management-service

spec:

  type: ClusterIP

  ports:
```

```
- port: 5002

targetPort: 5002

selector:

app: course-management
```

This service ensures that the Course Management service can be discovered and accessed by other services within the cluster using Kubernetes' built-in DNS. This setup not only enhances operational efficiency but also improves the reliability and scalability of the overall university application architecture.

Deploying Python Applications on AWS

When you use Amazon Web Services (AWS) to deploy your Python apps, you gain access to a scalable cloud computing environment that can handle all the different requirements of a university app with ease. From basic Elastic Compute Cloud (EC2) instances to more advanced orchestrated environments with ECS and EKS, AWS provides a wide range of services for application deployment and management.

Setting up AWS for University Application

Before deploying the application, you need to set up an AWS account and configure the necessary services.

Create an AWS Account

If you haven't already, sign up for an AWS account at aws.amazon.com. Once you have your account, log in to the AWS Management Console.

Setup IAM (Identity and Access Management)

For security, it's important to manage AWS resources using IAM:

1. Create a new IAM user:
   o Navigate to the IAM dashboard within the AWS Console.
   o Choose "Users" from the sidebar and click "Add user".
   o Set a user name and select "Programmatic access" as the access type.
   o Follow prompts to attach policies directly or add the user to a group with appropriate permissions.

2. Secure your root and IAM user with MFA (Multi-Factor Authentication):

   o On the IAM dashboard, select your IAM user.

   o Under the "Security credentials" tab, beside "Assigned MFA device", click "Manage" and follow the instructions to add MFA.

Configure AWS CLI

Install the AWS CLI on your local machine to interact with AWS services directly from your terminal:

```
pip install awscli

aws configure
```

Enter your AWS Access Key ID, Secret Access Key, region, and output format when prompted.

Deploying the Application on AWS

For deploying a Python application, you can use either Elastic Beanstalk for an automated deployment process or EC2 for more control.

Option 1: Using Elastic Beanstalk

1. AWS Elastic Beanstalk simplifies the deployment and scaling of applications:

   o Ensure your application has a **requirements.txt** file at the root, detailing all necessary Python packages.

   o Include a **Procfile** to specify the commands that are executed by the application's containers on startup, e.g., **web: python app.py**.

2. Deploy using Elastic Beanstalk:

   o Install the Elastic Beanstalk CLI.

   o Navigate to your project directory and run:

```
eb init -p python-3.8 my-university-app --region your-
aws-region

eb create my-university-app-env
```

This will set up Elastic Beanstalk, which handles deployment, from capacity provisioning, load balancing, auto-scaling to application health monitoring.

Option 2: Using EC2

If you require more control over the server:

1. Launch an EC2 Instance:

    o   In the AWS Console, go to the EC2 dashboard and click "Launch Instance".

    o   Choose an appropriate AMI (Amazon Machine Image), like Ubuntu Server.

    o   Select instance type, configure instance details, add storage, add tags, configure security group, and review.

2. SSH into Your Instance:

    o   Once the instance is running, connect to it using SSH with your private key.

```
ssh -i "your-key-pair.pem" ubuntu@ec2-your-instance-
public-dns.amazonaws.com
```

3. Set up the Environment:

    o   Install Python, pip, and other dependencies.

    o   Clone your repository or transfer your application files to the instance.

    o   Set up a web server like Nginx or Apache to serve your application.

Whether you prefer EC2's control and flexibility or Elastic Beanstalk's automated management features, AWS offers robust tools to help you deploy complicated applications.

Using Serverless Architectures with AWS Lambda

Understanding AWS Lambda

We can optimize and simplify the deployment of certain features in our university app using serverless architectures, especially AWS Lambda, which reduces operational overhead and scaling costs compared to traditional server-based setups. AWS Lambda is a compute service that lets you run code without provisioning or managing servers. You pay only for the compute time you consume - there is no charge when your code is not running. With Lambda, you can run code for virtually any type of application or backend service with zero administration. AWS Lambda executes your code only when needed and scales automatically. Without adding or managing servers, AWS Lambda lets you run code in response to events like HTTP requests through API Gateway, changes in data in DynamoDB, or changes in state in S3 buckets.

Setting up AWS Lambda

To use AWS Lambda for parts of the university application, you first need to set up the necessary AWS environment and prepare your application for deployment.

Prepare your Application

Suppose we have a Python function to handle student registration, which is a good candidate for serverless due to its event-driven nature (e.g., triggered by registration form submissions).

- Create a lambda_function.py:
    - This file will contain the function that AWS Lambda will execute.

```python
import json


def lambda_handler(event, context):
  # Assume `event` contains registration details
  student = event['body']
  # Process registration
  registration_status = process_registration(student)
  return {
  'statusCode': 200,
  'body': json.dumps({
  'message': 'Registration successful',
  'details': registration_status
  })
  }


def process_registration(student):
```

```
# Logic to register the student

return "Student registered."
```

- Package Dependencies:
    - If your function depends on external libraries, package them with your deployment package.

```
pip install --target ./package requests

cd package

zip -r ../my-deployment-package.zip .

cd ..

zip -g my-deployment-package.zip lambda_function.py
```

Create Lambda Function in AWS

Log into the AWS Management Console and open the AWS Lambda console.

1. Create a new Lambda function:
    - Click "Create function".
    - Choose "Author from scratch".
    - Enter a function name.
    - Choose Python 3.8 for the runtime.
    - Set up permissions by choosing an existing role or creating a new one that has permissions to access the resources your function needs.
2. Upload Your Code:
    - In the "Function code" section, upload your zip file (**my-deployment-package.zip**).
    - Set the handler information (e.g., **lambda_function.lambda_handler**).
3. Configure Trigger:
    - Click "Add trigger".
    - Choose AWS API Gateway.
    - Create a new API or attach to an existing one.

- o Set the security to "Open" for testing.

4. Deploy and Test:

  - o Deploy your changes.

  - o Use the API Gateway URL provided to trigger your function via HTTP requests.

AWS Lambda can handle various aspects of the university application that are event-driven, such as sending notifications to students, processing enrollment requests, or integrating with other AWS services like DynamoDB for data storage or S3 for file management.

Each of these functionalities can be encapsulated into separate Lambda functions, making the system highly modular and reducing the load on the main application server. This not only improves scalability by allowing each function to scale independently based on demand but also optimizes costs, as you pay only for the compute time used.

Implementing gRPC for Microservices Communication

Need of gRPC

In a microservices architecture, efficient communication between services is crucial for the overall performance and reliability of the application. gRPC, developed by Google, is a high-performance, open-source universal RPC (Remote Procedure Call) framework that uses HTTP/2 for transport and Protocol Buffers as the interface description language. It is particularly suited for connecting services in a microservices architecture due to its support for multiple languages and its efficiency in connecting polyglot services across distributed systems. Traditional RESTful APIs over HTTP/1.1 can become a bottleneck due to their verbose text format and the overhead of opening and closing connections. gRPC addresses these issues by using HTTP/2, which supports multiplexing many requests over a single connection, and by transmitting data in a binary format, which makes serialization and deserialization much faster.

Implementing gRPC in Python Microservices

To implement gRPC in the university application, where we have already defined several microservices like admissions, course management, and student records, follow these steps:

Define Service using Protocol Buffers

First, define the gRPC service and the method request and response types using protocol buffers. Create a **.proto** file for each service interaction.

For instance, let's define a simple service for the Course Management microservice:

```
// course_management.proto
syntax = "proto3";


package coursemanagement;


// The course management service definition.
service CourseManagement {
  // Sends a greeting
  rpc GetCourseDetails (CourseRequest) returns
(CourseResponse) {}
}


// The request message containing the course ID.
message CourseRequest {
  string course_id = 1;
}


// The response message containing course details.
message CourseResponse {
  string course_id = 1;
  string title = 2;
  string description = 3;
  int32 credits = 4;
```

```
}
```

Generate Server and Client Code

Use the protocol buffer compiler to generate client and server stubs from your **.proto** files.

```
python -m grpc_tools.protoc -I. --python_out=. --
grpc_python_out=. course_management.proto
```

This command generates **course_management_pb2.py** and **course_management_pb2_grpc.py**, which contain the classes for the request and response messages, and the server and client classes, respectively.

Implement the Service in Python

Implement the server-side logic for handling a gRPC request.

```python
from concurrent import futures

import grpc

import course_management_pb2

import course_management_pb2_grpc


class
CourseManagementServicer(course_management_pb2_grpc.Cours
eManagementServicer):
  def GetCourseDetails(self, request, context):
  response = course_management_pb2.CourseResponse()
  course_id = request.course_id
  # Simulate fetching course details from the database.
  response.course_id = course_id
  response.title = "Introduction to Microservices"
```

```python
    response.description = "Learn the basics of
microservices architecture."

    response.credits = 3

    return response


def serve():
    server =
grpc.server(futures.ThreadPoolExecutor(max_workers=10))

course_management_pb2_grpc.add_CourseManagementServicer_t
o_server(

    CourseManagementServicer(), server)

    server.add_insecure_port('[::]:50051')

    server.start()

    server.wait_for_termination()


if __name__ == '__main__':

    serve()
```

Create the Client

The client code will call the service defined by the server.

```python
import grpc

import course_management_pb2

import course_management_pb2_grpc
```

```python
def run():

    with grpc.insecure_channel('localhost:50051') as
channel:

        stub =
course_management_pb2_grpc.CourseManagementStub(channel)

        response =
stub.GetCourseDetails(course_management_pb2.CourseRequest
(course_id='CS101'))

        print("Course retrieved: ", response.title)


if __name__ == '__main__':

    run()
```

The gRPC protocol is essential for ensuring data consistency and enhancing the efficiency of operations in a microservices architecture. This above example shows how to set up a simple gRPC server and client inside the microservices, which can be used as a starting point for adding more services to the application.

Summary

In this chapter, we explored the advanced concepts of microservices and cloud integration, with an emphasis on how to optimize the Python architecture and deployment strategies for the university application. The first steps were to plan and construct microservices. The admissions, course management, and student records components of the university application were decomposed into smaller, independent services. This approach made it easier to manage and scale.

These microservices were managed with the help of Docker and Kubernetes, demonstrating how containerization streamlines microservices deployment and orchestration. For portability and consistency across environments, we containerized each microservice using Docker. The orchestration of these containers, including management of their lifecycle, scaling, and state preservation, was then performed by Kubernetes.

Cloud environments, and more especially AWS, became the focal point of deployment strategies. Elastic Beanstalk and Elastic Compute Cloud (EC2) were both showcased in the chapter as useful AWS services for automating Python application deployments and providing more control and customization options. In addition, we learned how to use AWS Lambda in serverless architectures. This method improved operational efficiency by allowing certain application functionalities, like handling registration events, to be handled without the burden of server provisioning and scaling.

Lastly, the chapter delved into how gRPC can be utilized to facilitate effective communication amongst microservices. As an efficient replacement for conventional REST APIs, gRPC enhanced communication between distributed services by making use of HTTP/2 and Protocol Buffers. All things considered, this chapter taught us to design and build a strong, scalable backend with the help of current tools and techniques, so the university app could adapt to changing loads and stay online in any setting.

CHAPTER 10: MESSAGE BROKERS AND ASYNCHRONOUS TASK PROCESSING

Introduction

In this chapter, we will look at how message brokers and asynchronous task processing are essential components of contemporary application architectures, especially for dealing with scalable and highly reliable operations. A wide range of methods and resources necessary for efficient asynchronous communication and project management are covered in detail in this chapter.

To begin, the chapter provides a high-level introduction to message brokers, outlining how they mediate communication and data transfer among application components and why they are important for decoupling them. Applications' adaptability, scalability, and modularity are all boosted by this configuration.

Kafka, a well-liked distributed streaming platform, is integrated later in the chapter after the introduction. It is particularly good at processing data in real-time. It explains how the university app can use Kafka to manage high-throughput data streams, which will allow for analytics and decisions to be made in real-time. The focus moves to Celery, a distributed task queue system that works with RabbitMQ and Redis to handle background tasks, as the topic continues to asynchronous task processing. In this chapter, you will learn how to configure and utilize Celery to handle long-running processes in a way that doesn't impede the main thread of the application, making it more responsive. Continuing our exploration of message brokers, we present RabbitMQ as an additional strong choice for managing asynchronous tasks. To help readers understand RabbitMQ's unique advantages and suitability for different scenarios, the chapter compares its features and capabilities with other brokers.

To sum up, this chapter gives readers the tools they need to construct efficient and scalable systems by teaching them how to integrate asynchronous task processing and message brokering into their products.

Message Brokers Overview

Message brokers play a pivotal role in modern backend architectures by facilitating effective communication between different parts of an application, especially in distributed systems. These brokers manage and mediate messages between service senders and receivers, ensuring data is reliably transferred without direct linkage of the components, which promotes a modular architecture.

Role of Message Brokers in Backend Applications

Message brokers are middleware that handle the transmission of messages between different components of an application. They are crucial in scenarios involving microservices architectures, where services must communicate asynchronously and remain loosely coupled.

The key functions of a message broker include:

1. Decoupling of Application Components: Message brokers allow different parts of an application to communicate without being directly connected, reducing dependencies and facilitating easier scalability and maintenance.

2. Asynchronous Communication: They enable asynchronous processing by allowing components to queue messages without waiting for responses, enhancing application responsiveness and efficiency.

3. Load Balancing: Brokers can distribute tasks or messages across multiple consumers in a balanced manner, optimizing resource use and improving the overall performance of the system.

4. Fault Tolerance: By decoupling services, message brokers help isolate failures in one part of the system from others. They often support message persistence, ensuring that messages are not lost in case of processing failures.

5. Guaranteed Delivery: Most message brokers support mechanisms that ensure messages are not lost — delivered at least once, or exactly once — crucial for critical transaction data.

Redis as a Message Broker

Redis, traditionally known for its role as an in-memory data store, also functions effectively as a message broker through its support for various data structures like lists, sets, and sorted sets, which can be used to implement queues for message delivery.

How Redis Facilitates Messaging?

Redis provides two primary mechanisms for handling messages: Pub/Sub (Publish/Subscribe) and persistent queues. While Pub/Sub in Redis does not guarantee message persistence (if a message is published and there are no subscribers, the message is lost), it is incredibly fast and simple for scenarios where delivery guarantees are not critical.

Following is the example using Redis in Python:

```
import redis


# Connecting to Redis

r = redis.Redis(host='localhost', port=6379, db=0)


# Publisher
```

```python
r.publish('emailChannel', 'Send welcome email to
user@gitforgits.com')


# Subscriber

pubsub = r.pubsub()

pubsub.subscribe('emailChannel')

for message in pubsub.listen():

 print(message)
```

Using Lists as Queues:

- Pushing messages: Components can push messages to a Redis list, which serves as a queue.
- Popping messages: Components can pop messages from the list for processing.

Following is the example:

```python
# Producer

r.lpush('taskQueue', 'task1')


# Consumer

task = r.rpop('taskQueue')

if task:

 print(f"Processing {task.decode('utf-8')}")
```

In our university application, Redis can be employed as a message broker to handle tasks like sending notifications to students, enrolling students into courses, or even for inter-service communication in a microservices architecture. For instance, when a new course is added through the Course Management Service, it could publish a message to a Redis channel, which the Notification Service is subscribed to, in order to alert students about the new course availability.

Integrating Kafka for Real-time Data Processing

Understanding Apache Kafka

Kafka operates on a cluster of one or more servers (brokers) and organizes messages in topics. Each message within a topic consists of a key, a value, and a timestamp. Kafka is highly durable and resilient to node failures and supports automatic recovery. Its performance does not significantly degrade as data size increases, making it ideal for applications with massive data streams like telemetry or logging data from multiple sources.

Core Components of Kafka

- Producer: Any application that publishes data (writes) to Kafka topics.

- Broker: A server in the Kafka cluster that stores data and serves clients.

- Topic: A category or feed to which records are published. Topics in Kafka are multi-subscriber; they can have zero, one, or many consumers that subscribe to the data.

- Consumer: Applications or processes that subscribe to (read) topics and process the feed of published messages.

- Zookeeper: Manages and coordinates Kafka brokers. It is essential for managing the state of the cluster.

Integrating Kafka for Real-Time Data Processing

We'll go over the steps to configure Kafka so that the university app can handle enrollment requests and dynamically update course availability in real time.

Setting up Kafka

- Start by downloading Kafka from the official Apache Kafka website and extract it. Kafka uses Zookeeper to manage and coordinate brokers. Start Zookeeper with the following command:

```
bin/zookeeper-server-start.sh config/zookeeper.properties
```

- After Zookeeper is running, start the Kafka server:

```
bin/kafka-server-start.sh config/server.properties
```

Creating Topics

Create a topic named "course-enrollment" that your application will use to process enrollment requests.

```
bin/kafka-topics.sh --create --topic course-enrollment --
bootstrap-server localhost:9092 --replication-factor 1 --
partitions 1
```

Implement Kafka Producers and Consumers

Assume we need to handle real-time course enrollments and send notifications.

- Producer Code: This part of the application sends messages to Kafka whenever a student enrolls in a course.

```
from kafka import KafkaProducer

import json


producer =
KafkaProducer(bootstrap_servers=['localhost:9092'],

 value_serializer=lambda v: json.dumps(v).encode('utf-
8'))


def send_enrollment(enrollment_info):

 producer.send('course-enrollment', enrollment_info)

 producer.flush()


send_enrollment({'student_id': 123, 'course_id':
'CS101'})
```

- Consumer Code: This part reads the enrollment messages and processes them, such as updating a database or triggering other actions.

```python
from kafka import KafkaConsumer

import json


consumer = KafkaConsumer('course-enrollment',
 bootstrap_servers=['localhost:9092'],
 auto_offset_reset='earliest',
 value_deserializer=lambda x: json.loads(x.decode('utf-
8')))


for message in consumer:
 enrollment_info = message.value
 print(f"Received enrollment info: {enrollment_info}")
 # Process the enrollment, e.g., update the database,
send notifications, etc.
```

For situations requiring low latency and high throughput, like processing student enrollments or updating course details across departments, Kafka is the way to go because of its scalability and ability to manage massive amounts of data. The scripts for producers and consumers make it possible to process data asynchronously, which keeps the application responsive and efficient.

Asynchronous Task Processing with Celery

Introduction to Asynchronous Task Processing

Asynchronous task processing involves executing tasks concurrently with application processes, typically on separate threads or processes, so that the main application can continue running smoothly. Asynchronous task processing is a crucial technique in modern applications, allowing them to perform long or resource-intensive operations in the background without blocking the main application flow. This method is especially beneficial for operations like sending batch emails, processing files, or generating reports, which might otherwise take a significant amount of time and degrade user experience if run synchronously.

Using Celery for Asynchronous Task Processing

Celery is a powerful, flexible asynchronous task queue/job queue based on distributed message passing. It is focused on real-time operation but supports scheduling as well. The execution units, called tasks, are executed concurrently on one or more worker nodes using multiprocessing, Eventlet, or gevent. Celery communicates via messages, usually using a broker to mediate between clients and workers.

How Celery Works?

We have already learned about Celery in one of the previous chapters but we will briefly understand it again its key components and how it works altogether:

Celery communicates with the queue through a message broker, such as RabbitMQ or Redis. The broker holds the queue of tasks that are to be executed. Worker processes constantly monitor the message broker and execute the tasks as they appear in the queue. Celery can store or send back the results of tasks using a backend like Redis, MongoDB, or AMQP.

Implementing Celery

Install Celery and Redis

First, just reconfirm that Celery and Redis are installed.

```
pip install celery redis
```

Configure Celery

Create a new file called **celery_app.py** in your university application directory. This file will configure the Celery application.

```
from celery import Celery


app = Celery('university_tasks',
 broker='redis://localhost:6379/0',
 backend='redis://localhost:6379/0')


@app.task
```

```python
def send_email(student_email, message):
 # Simulate sending an email
 print(f"Sending email to {student_email} with message: {message}")
 return 'Email sent'


@app.task
def process_enrollment(course_id, student_id):
 # Simulate processing enrollment
 print(f"Processing enrollment for student {student_id} to course {course_id}")
 return 'Enrollment processed'
```

Running Celery Worker

To execute the tasks, you need to run a Celery worker from your project directory.

```
celery -A celery_app worker --loglevel=info
```

This command starts a Celery worker that listens for tasks in the Redis queue and processes them as they arrive.

Queueing Tasks

From another part of your application or from a separate script, you can now queue tasks to be processed by the worker.

```python
from celery_app import send_email, process_enrollment


# Queue a task to send an email
```

```
send_email.delay('student@gitforgits.com', 'Welcome to
the course!')
```

```
# Queue a task to process enrollment

process_enrollment.delay('CS101', '12345')
```

The **.delay()** method is used to send tasks to the broker asynchronously, which are then picked up by the worker.

In this configuration, complicated operations, such as sending email notifications or enrolling students, can run in the background without slowing down the application for end users.

RabbitMQ as Alternative Message Broker

Particularly in microservices or event-driven paradigm architectures, message brokers are vital for managing data exchange and communication between components of distributed systems. Their dependable message queuing, delivery, and processing, as well as their ability to decouple application components, can result in systems that are easier to scale and maintain. While Kafka and Redis are well-known choices, RabbitMQ is a strong alternative with extensive messaging capabilities.

Understanding RabbitMQ and Its Necessity

RabbitMQ is an open-source message broker that is known for its reliability, flexibility, and support for multiple messaging protocols, including AMQP (Advanced Message Queuing Protocol). It offers a variety of features like message queuing, delivery acknowledgment, flexible routing, and transactions, making it a strong choice for complex applications that require robust message delivery mechanisms, such as order processing systems, banking transactions, or real-time data processing systems.

The necessity of an alternative message broker like RabbitMQ in the backend architecture of any application arises from the need to handle high throughput and reliable message delivery in a distributed environment. RabbitMQ provides these capabilities and ensures that messages are not lost even in the case of consumer failures, which is crucial for critical business processes.

Integrating RabbitMQ

What if we assume our university application requires reliable message handling for events like registration notifications, course updates, or even administrative commands that need to be propagated through various parts of the system reliably.

Install RabbitMQ

First, ensure that RabbitMQ is installed on your system. RabbitMQ can be installed on various operating systems and also offers a Docker image.

For a basic installation on Ubuntu, you can use the following commands:

```
sudo apt update

sudo apt install rabbitmq-server

sudo systemctl enable rabbitmq-server

sudo systemctl start rabbitmq-server
```

You can then enable the management interface for easier handling:

```
sudo rabbitmq-plugins enable rabbitmq_management
```

Set up RabbitMQ in the Application

With RabbitMQ running, the next step is to integrate it into the university application using Celery, which we previously configured to work with Redis.

Update your **celery_app.py** to use RabbitMQ as the broker. Change the broker URL to point to RabbitMQ:

```
from celery import Celery


app = Celery('university_tasks',
  broker='amqp://user:password@localhost/',
  backend='rpc://')


@app.task
def send_notification(message):
  print(f"Notification: {message}")
```

```
    return "Notification sent"


@app.task

def process_registration(details):

  print(f"Registration details: {details}")

  return "Registration processed"
```

In the above code snippet, **amqp://user:password@localhost/** is the default connection string for RabbitMQ. Replace **user** and **password** with the appropriate credentials.

Start a Celery worker that will listen for messages from RabbitMQ:

```
celery -A celery_app worker --loglevel=info
```

Sending Messages

With Celery and RabbitMQ configured, you can enqueue tasks from anywhere within your application:

```
from celery_app import send_notification,
process_registration


# Enqueue tasks

send_notification.delay("New course available!")

process_registration.delay("Student John Doe has
registered for Physics 101.")
```

When advanced routing capabilities and message delivery guarantees are needed in complex systems, RabbitMQ is a significant choice due to its robustness.

Summary

This chapter explored the complexities of message brokers and asynchronous task processing, breaking down their roles in improving the performance of backend applications. This is particularly true when dealing with complicated operations that require scalability and reliability. A comprehensive introduction to message brokers was provided in the first section of the chapter, outlining their critical function in enabling strong communication amongst components of distributed applications. Overall application efficiency and reliability are both improved by this setup, which decouples system parts and streamlines data flow across processes.

Apache Kafka, with its strengths in real-time data processing, was the next topic of learnings in this chapter. Given its demonstrated ability to manage high-throughput data streams, Kafka is well-suited to situations requiring rapid processing and responsiveness, like the university system's handling of real-time transactional data.

In addition, Celery, a task queue, was presented in the chapter. It collaborates with RabbitMQ and Redis, two message brokers, to effectively handle background tasks. The university app was able to keep its user interface responsive thanks to Celery's integration, which offloaded intensive tasks like sending bulk emails or processing user data requests asynchronously.

Finally, we moved on to learn about RabbitMQ, an alternate message broker with powerful message queuing features. Critical applications that cannot afford message loss will find its robustness and reliability in handling messages particularly valuable. The integration of RabbitMQ into the university application improved its communication and task processing management capabilities.

Epilogue

Having completed "Practical Python Backend Programming," I hope you have a better grasp of the subject and the tools necessary to dive headfirst into the Python world of backend development. The journey through this book is intended to inspire a deliberate approach to developing software that is reliable, scalable, and secure in addition to teaching the technicalities and tools that make for efficient backend systems.

From the very beginning of Python programming to more advanced topics such as database integration, asynchronous processing, and security, we have covered it all throughout the chapters. We have also covered web frameworks such as Flask and FastAPI. An integrated learning experience that reflects the real-world progression of software development projects was achieved by meticulously crafting each section to build upon the previous one. The goal in going through these examples and projects was to give you some real-world experience and information that you can use for your own development projects. We aimed to show you the ropes of backend development, from creating a development environment to deploying apps to the cloud, so you can be ready for the decisions and challenges you'll encounter on the job.

Keep in mind that technology is a dynamic field that is always changing as you progress. Although the methods and tools we've covered are state-of-the-art, maintaining a constant hunger for knowledge is essential for every successful developer. It is my hope that you will continue to seek out new information, try out different technologies, and polish your abilities.

Engage in communities, make contributions to open source projects, and perpetuate the cycle of knowledge sharing. Your knowledge and skills as a developer will be enhanced by participating in these activities. The people they introduce you to will share your interests and provide you with companionship, advice, and support.

If there's one thing I hope you've learned from this book, it's how to approach backend projects strategically. As important as it is to write code, programming is primarily about finding solutions to problems. Every line you write contributes to something bigger, whether it's an internal tool with a few thousand users or a system with millions of users.

Last but not least, I want to thank you for following this book as your path to knowledge and for your dedication to learning. Sharing what I've learned with you has been a great privilege. Although becoming an expert backend developer is no picnic, the payoff is well worth the effort. Never stop learning, never stop pushing yourself, and, above all, never stop enjoying the creative and innovative process.

Thank You

Made in the USA
Las Vegas, NV
22 October 2024

10273181R00144